CONTENTS

FOREWORD

Not too long ago, formal education in the Republic of Ireland was characterised by a predominance of religious influences at all levels. For instance, we can identify the following as strong and traditional features of the educational system until the seventies, and in the case of some of these, until much more recently: the prevalence of religious in the principalships of post-primary schools and the plentiful supply of religious among the ranks of teachers; the almost exclusive control of the management of primary schools by ecclesiastical authorities; the regular conduct of religious practices in schools, including liturgies and preparation for sacraments; the importance given to religion as a subject of study in the curriculum of the primary school ('Of all the parts of a school curriculum, Religious Instruction is by far the most important' [Primary Curriculum 1971]); the control of teacher training colleges by Church authorities and the denominational nature of that control; the denominational character of most schooling at both primary and second levels; the far-reaching constraints placed on theological research by episcopal authorities; the preponderance of religious in senior positions in the philosophy and social sciences departments of the universities in the NUI system; the ban on Catholics attending Trinity College Dublin; the high proportion of chairmanships of VECs occupied by clerical figures; the tendency of State authorities to bow to Church influences where philosophical issues in education were concerned.

This list is not exhaustive, but it is sufficient to illustrate the extent to which religious influences permeated the Irish educational system, and to give some indication of the frequently paternalistic nature of these influences. Some of these features have completely disappeared. Others still exist in a modified form. The notable decline of a religious presence in schools in

5

recent years and the rapid rise of secular and pluralist influences have dramatically altered many of the historical patterns of Irish schooling. Lay teachers now hold, or aspire to, positions of leadership in both primary and post-primary education on a wide scale. Increasing numbers of pupils betray attitudes which seem indifferent or inhospitable to religion. In addition, traditional conceptions of authority and obedience within religious life have undergone many changes. The picture continues to change rapidly, moreover, and often in a way which challenges the kinds of assumptions underlying the powers and prerogatives long enjoyed by the Churches in education. When the traditional background is considered in the light of the changes taking place at present, it seems likely that the rationale for religion in Irish education in the future will be very different from what the accepted pattern was in the past.

Bearing all of this in mind, it is strange that religion featured only in a minor way in the Government's publications *Education for a Changing World* (Green Paper 1992) and *Charting our Education Future* (White Paper 1995). Of course it featured in a much more central way during the deliberations of the National Education Convention in 1993 and in the subsequent negotiations. Yet, the manner in which religion came to the fore in these discussions had more to do with efforts to secure legal guarantees than with the question of a coherent rationale for the place of religion in the educational system of the future. In other words, the concerns of religious authorities themselves during the national educational debate seemed to focus rather more on managerial rights and powers than on the quality of the religious influences actually experienced by pupils in schools.

Apart from the notable contributions of the Conference of Major Religious Superiors (now the Conference of Religious of Ireland), a striking feature of the debate itself was the lack of attention by the main 'partners' during the continuing national education debate to this basic question of a rationale for religion in our rapidly changing education system.[1] It prompted the Educational Studies Association of Ireland to join forces with two other voluntary associations, the Irish Theological Association and the Religion Teachers' Association, to provide a public forum to explore some of the chief aspects of such a rationale. That forum was a two-day conference held in Dublin in February 1996. Like all conferences organised under ESAI auspices it was governed by the norms of academic freedom, so contributors were invited to speak primarily from the perspective of their own research and experience rather than as spokespersons for various groups or institutions. The conference drew a packed house from throughout the country to the large amphitheatre in St Patrick's College, Drumcondra. It included incisive and plentiful contributions from the wide range of participants, as well as from the invited speakers.

The conference proceedings, including its discussion sessions and concluding symposium, were recorded. During the final session of the conference the opinions of participants were sought on the possible publication of the proceedings. The unanimous view of those present was that the issues considered by the conference were of major importance to the quality of education in Ireland in the years ahead and would be of deep interest to colleagues in all parts of the country who could not be present in Dublin for the conference. The organisers were strongly urged to publish the proceedings and this book is offered primarily in response to these wishes. The editors hope, moreover, that it will enable a much wider range of people to share in the richness of the deliberations at Drumcondra. To do so is to take an active and purposeful part in the current historical transformation of one of the most significant features of the Irish educational system.

A few words are called for on the editorial procedures employed in preparing the book. In some cases, speakers submitted the texts of their contributions after the conference, and in others the text was transcribed from the records made. In all cases however, the final text of each of the main contributions has been approved by the speaker in question. This is also true of the responses by the speakers to questions and comments from the floor. In addition to the contributions from the speakers listed on the programme for the conference the book contains two further papers. The first of these is the opening paper, an important and illuminating exploration by Kevin Williams of the legal and policy framework for religion in Irish education. The second is the closing paper, a thought-provoking 'afterword' contributed by Dermot Lane at the invitation of the editors. This 'afterword' provides food for thought for educators and policy-makers alike and is itself an invitation to envisage religious education, and indeed religious influences in education, as abiding sources of light and hope in an age when the shifting concerns and tastes of the market have pervaded all aspects of culture; sources indeed which were all too often eclipsed by distorted conceptions of religion embodied in some of our inherited educational traditions. The editors are deeply grateful to Dr Lane for his perceptive and timely observations.

Special thanks are due to the speakers for their willingness to accept the invitation to contribute and for putting forward their viewpoints in an engaging, insightful and open-hearted way: to Dr Michael Paul Gallagher SJ, Gregorian University Rome; Rev Michael Drumm, Mater Dei Institute, Dublin; Ann Walsh, CBS Kilkenny and NCCA; Kieran Griffin, Bray School Project National School; Tom Larkin, Scoil Cholmcille, Donaghamede. Thanks are also due to the chairpersons of the two discussion sessions and symposium: Dr Geraldine Smyth OP, Irish School of Ecumenics; Anne Looney, Assumption Secondary School, Walkinstown, and NCCA; Dr Joseph Dunne, St Patrick's College, Drumcondra. The editors would also like to express their appreciation to Dr Donal Harrington and Pádraig Conway of the Irish Theological Association and to Robert Dunne of the

Religion Teachers' Association for their joint efforts with the ESAI in organising the conference. Finally, a special word of thanks to Anne Marie Kieran, Mater Dei Institute, whose unfailing attention to the roving microphone ensured that all of the conference proceedings, including those contributions from the more remote parts of the amphitheatre, were available on tape for transcription. These many contributions from the floor make this book a much more inclusive colloquium than would otherwise have been possible.

Pádraig Hogan
Maynooth College
March 1997

1

RELIGION IN IRISH EDUCATION: RECENT TRENDS IN GOVERNMENT POLICY

Kevin Williams

The status of religious education in schools in Ireland is complex and its treatment in recent government documents, principally the Green Paper 1992, *Education for a Changing World,* and the White Paper of 1995, *Charting our Education Future,* reflects this complexity.[1] This chapter considers the trend of official policy with regard to (1) the role of religion in schools in general and the place of religious education in particular; (2) the relationship between religious education and curricular areas such as health education and civics.

Religion and Religious Education

The tone of the Green Paper in its treatment of religion is very different from that of previous documents such as *The Primary Teacher's Handbook* and *The Rules for National Schools.* Where matters of religion and spirituality are mentioned in the Green Paper, they are treated in a dispassionate tone as aspects of a culture which merit being critically understood rather than assimilated in any formative sense. In this perspective we read of 'fostering an understanding and critical appreciation of the values – moral, spiritual, social and cultural – of the home and society generally' and of aiming to 'develop' in young people 'an understanding of their own religious beliefs and a tolerance for the beliefs of others'.[2] Consistent with this emphasis is a tendency to interpret religious education narrowly in terms of instruction in a religious faith. This means that the implications of belief for general values education and for the full personal development of young people are overlooked.

By contrast, the tone of the White Paper with regard to religious education is more balanced, nuanced and sensitive than that of the Green Paper. Whereas the Green Paper refers to the aim of 'fostering an understanding and critical appreciation of the values – moral, spiritual, social and cultural – of the home and society generally', the White Paper speaks of fostering an 'understanding and critical appreciation of the values – moral spiritual, religious, social and cultural – which have been distinctive in shaping Irish society and which have been traditionally accorded respect in society'.[3] The change in tone is also marked in the treatment of the role of religious education at junior cycle of secondary school. The Green Paper states that 'religious education should form part of the available programme for all students, with due regard to the constitutional rights of parents related to the participation of their children'.[4] The objective of the White Paper, on the other hand, is that by the end of junior cycle/compulsory schooling 'all students, in accordance with their abilities and aptitudes', will have enjoyed 'formative experiences in moral, religious and spiritual education'.[5] Religious education is included as one of the areas which 'each school will be expected to provide'[6] and no reference is made to the right of parents to withdraw their children from religious education. No doubt this right is assumed but the authors of the White Paper reasonably felt that it was unnecessary to labour the obvious. Although the White Paper does not refer to the status of religion at senior cycle, this is consistent with the treatment of the standard curriculum for the Leaving Certificate where the role of individual subjects is not explored. Yet, in so far as provision 'at senior cycle will be characterised by continuity with and progression from junior cycle'[7], there could be said to be an implied recognition of the place of religious education at this level.

The right to withdraw from religious education

Although already enshrined in the Constitution and endorsed in Department of Education documents, the right of non-believing parents to withdraw their children from religious education is a preoccupation in both documents, although, as noted above, the issue is less laboured in the White Paper. In the section of the Green Paper dealing with religious education in the primary school, this right is asserted explicitly and forcefully several times. Concern is expressed that

> changes in the *Rules for National Schools* over time, and embodied in the Rules published in 1965, could be seen to have the effect of weakening the protections that existed for children of religious beliefs different from those of the majority in the schools.[8]

Here the authors are probably referring to the requirement of teachers to be careful in the presence of children of different religious beliefs not to touch on issues of controversy, which was removed from Rule 68 in the 1965 edition of *Rules for National Schools*. The passage then continues:

> The general review of the *Rules for National Schools,* recommended by the Primary Education Review Body, will seek also to ensure that all aspects of the *Rules* fully reflect the relevant articles of the Constitution. Furthermore, the 1971 *Teachers' Handbook for the Primary School,* as part of its promotion of an integrated curriculum, also sought to integrate religious and secular instruction. The *Handbook* will be reviewed to ensure that the constitutional rights of children are fully safeguarded.[9]

But what is not stated is whether the changes envisaged would simply involve the removal of the reference to the centrality of religion in the primary curriculum and of the requirement that religion serve as a important element in curriculum integration, or whether overt reference to religion would be prohibited outside of the time set aside for religious instruction.

The rights of non-believing parents were also considered in the *Report on the National Education Convention* which notes, for example, that where parents withdraw their children from religion class, this may have 'peer-stigmatising effects'.[10] The general thrust of the treatment of the issue in the *Report on the National Education Convention* is reflected in the White Paper, which reaffirms

> **the right of schools in accordance with their religious ethos, to provide denominational religious education and instruction to their students** while underpinning the constitutional rights of parents to withdraw their children from religious education instruction (emphasis in original).[11]

The document also reaffirms the commitment to ensure that 'the Constitutional rights of children are fully safeguarded' and to review the *Rules for National Schools* and the *Teachers' Handbook* in revising the primary curriculum.[12] In this perspective, the Department of Education will require all schools to 'ensure that the rights of those who do not subscribe to the school's ethos are protected in a caring manner'.[13] The document shows particular concern that a balance be struck between the

> rights, obligations and choices of the majority of parents and students, who subscribe to the ethos of a school, and those of a minority, who may not subscribe to that ethos, but who do not have the option, for practical reasons, to select a school which reflects their particular choices.[14]

The issue is raised again in the final chapter of the document which examines the legal and constitutional framework for education. It is argued that the denominational character of schools

> must be reasonable and proportionate to the legitimate aim of preserving the ethos of schools and must balance this right of schools and their students against the rights to education of students of different denominations or none and the rights of teachers to earn a livelihood.[15]

Accordingly it proposes that a working party be established to develop the 'good practice' guidelines recommended by the *Report on the National Education Convention.*[16]

While no one would wish to deny parents their constitutional right to withdraw their children from religious education, the exercise of this right does ignore any possible right which young people might be said to have to an education in religion in any formative sense. This means that if the children of non-believing parents are not exposed to religion in school, they may never encounter religion as a significant source of meaning in human life. This is not the place to address this very large issue. Yet there is a need to consider the appropriate balance between the rights of parents, the rights of children and the duty of educators to ensure that the education of young people in their charge is as comprehensive as possible regarding the good in human life. And the rights of children must be to the fore in our discussions.

Religious, Personal, Social and Moral Education
Up to the present there has, unfortunately, been no clear consideration of the relationship between religious, moral, values education and health education. Until 1995, which saw the introduction of Relationships and Sexuality Education at both primary and secondary levels, there was no mandatory provision

for direct values education at primary level. At secondary level, the study of civics is compulsory for all junior cycle pupils but, regrettably, there has not been a tradition of taking the subject seriously and there are no requirements regarding the qualifications necessary to teach it. This has meant that general moral/values education of a formal nature has traditionally been included within the remit of religious education. In fact, it might be argued that the emphasis within religious education has become insufficiently theological due to the need to incorporate subject matter which more appropriately belongs in civics and in programmes of personal and social development. This tendency has been reinforced by the non-examined status of religious education. Many schools perceive religion class as the forum for the promotion of the personal development which it is not possible to provide within the constraints of the examination-driven curriculum.

Clarification of the relationship between religious education and personal, social and moral education will serve to highlight the constitutional obligation of the State to ensure that every pupil receives a 'certain minimum education, moral, intellectual and social' (Article 42). This will mean that formal provision will be required to secure the general moral education of pupils who are withdrawn from religious instruction. There is, however, much evidence that the trend of Government policy is to assign the broader remit of values education to health education. Both the Green Paper and White Paper appear to attribute to health education a main role in the formation of personal and social values. These values include what are referred to as 'spiritual' values. The promotion of health and well-being should occur within the context of 'the wider educational and spiritual values transmitted by the school'.[17] One of the elements mentioned under health promotion is sexuality education, which clearly involves consideration of values. The Green Paper lists a programme in sexuality education as one of the three defining features of the health-promoting school and it is recommended that it be provided at a level appropriate to all pupils beginning the early stages of primary education.[18] Health promotion in schools also has an explicit moral remit. The Green Paper speaks of helping students to 'become young persons who are honest, direct and self-confident, yet sensitive to the feelings and rights of others' and the White Paper speaks of fostering 'integrity, self-confidence and self-esteem while nurturing sensitivity to the feelings and rights of others'.[19]

Consistent with the policy of assigning the broader remit of values education to health education, in January 1995 formal arrangements were proposed for the teaching of Relationships and Sexuality Education (RSE) in primary and secondary schools. In the document introducing the new arrangements, the Minister for Education also announced that hours spent teaching RSE would count for salary purposes. It is interesting to note the high profile given to the moral and spiritual dimension of this aspect of education. The third paragraph of the document states:

> Through Relationships and Sexuality Education, formal opportunities are provided for young people to acquire knowledge and understanding of human sexuality, through processes which will enable them to form values and establish behaviours within a moral and spiritual framework.[20]

Further on the document states that RSE 'will be determined and delivered in accordance with the ethos and core values of the individual school'.[21] The document also asks that each school 'will make provision for the right of parents who hold conscientious or moral objections to the inclusion of such programmes on the curriculum' and requires of school authorities that they 'state how the school intends to address these situations'.[22]

The government is also expected to endorse proposals from the National Council for Curriculum and Assessment to improve the profile of civics in secondary schools.[23] The NCCA proposes that civics be subject to formal assessment and certification. The Council recommends the inclusion of structured cross-curricular activity, with time allocated to substantial project work. It also recommends that provision for civics be made at senior cycle, and that it be considered as an optional subject for the Leaving Certificate examination.

Examinations in religion

Another aspect of the Government policy towards religious education is to introduce religion as a subject for state examinations at secondary level.[24] This will require the repeal of a rule prohibiting examinations in religion. This rule is to be found in the Intermediate Education Act of 1878 which still provides the legal framework for secondary education in Ireland. Besides conferring on the subject a status which it does not currently enjoy, public examinations in religious education should have the somewhat paradoxical benefit of reinforcing the theological dimension of religious education. This is because the syllabus for examinations in religion can concentrate on conventional theological subject-matter rather than on material which can be covered in programmes of personal and social development. Of course, I would not wish to deny the implications of religious belief for moral education and for full personal development. But the primary concern of religious education is with the spiritual realm of human experience and its primary purpose is to enable young people to deepen their sensitivity and response to the transcendent action of God in their lives. In order to deepen the response of young people to the action of God in their lives, it is important to concentrate on subject-matter which is explicitly and directly theological rather than on material which would find a more appropriate place in civics or geography class or in programmes of personal and social development.

I shall conclude with some comments on the fear expressed by some that examinations in religion may result in religion being treated as simply another examination subject.[25] I am optimistic that the introduction of religion as an examination subject will not lead to the neglect of the non-examinable aspects of religious belief and practice. After all, there are State examinations in religion in Northern Ireland and it is unlikely that the catechetical formation of young people in the Northern part of the island is inferior to that in the Republic. The commitment of those who manage and teach in our schools makes me confident that our educators are not likely to mistake the study of religion for a genuine encounter with religion as an integral aspect of human living.

2

NEW FORMS OF CULTURAL UNBELIEF

Michael Paul Gallagher SJ

Cultural change

As early as 1958 Raymond Williams dared to say 'Culture is ordinary: that is the first fact' – in the sense that every society has its own purposes and meanings which it expresses in various ways and embodies in 'a whole way of life'.[1] This is one of three major meanings of culture that float around in our contemporary usage – culture as lived. The older meaning of creative culture also continues – pointing to the more conscious worlds of intellectual reflection, literary and artistic activity, and so on. A third meaning can be called local culture, especially in the sense of ethnic traditions often associated with smaller groupings of people. Whatever meaning is dominant, it is increasingly clear today that culture, in its various senses, offers a privileged field for watching received images undergo challenge and change.

Moreover, cultural change is something deeper and more complex than social change. It is like the difference between invisible and visible in the sense that social movements like urbanisation are relatively external whereas cultural movements involve many hidden factors of attitudes, inherited assumptions, indeed a whole implicit philosophy of existence. Therefore, when we talk of major cultural changes in recent decades, even though it is relatively easy to agree that major movements of sensibility are taking place, it is much harder to pinpoint exactly what is involved or what the long-term significance of such shifts is. Perhaps Thomas Kuhn's famous notion of paradigm shifts offers a better indicator of the nature of these cultural changes than a merely sociological analysis; a paradigm means a whole way of seeing and making sense of things, a cluster of beliefs and values shared by members of a community. When such interpretative models change, it is because the older approaches become not so much untrue as invalid, incapable of docking, so to speak, with new horizons of exploration. In similar fashion a culture involves a convergence of ways of seeing life, and when it changes, something more is happening than in the more visible social field. Cultural change means a paradigm shift in people's perceptions of their lives. Their horizons expand or contract, and hence subtle movements occur within their self-images and in their relationships. People carry around, so to speak, an often unacknowledged set of interpretative tools, ways of responding to existence: these instruments or lenses of seeing are at the centre of cultural change.

My topic is unbelief as a by-product of cultural change. It seems obvious that – in the western world in general – the typical tone of unbelief has moved from a sometimes militant denial of God to a more vague distance from religious faith. Some commentators describe this as the transition from the 'modern', with its trust in reason, human control and technology, to the 'post-modern', with its scepticism about large humanist claims and its corresponding mood of unease over any meanings and values. If the word 'atheism' tended to suggest a concrete decision, or a deliberate stance that rejects God, the very term 'unbelief' evokes less clarity and more confusion and doubt. Religious faith is not so much negated as sensed to be unreal and, taking the west in general, religious indifference or non-dogmatic agnosticism now seems to be the commonest form of unbelief. One has to add that in particular situations such as Ireland or Poland, the tones may remain more aggressive and less non-dogmatic. Agnosticism can express itself as a more vehement allergy against Church presence in education and public life, and because of the perceived power of the Church, some unbelievers in the fields of communications and education feel called to a crusade of total opposition or at least of overt despising of the religious dimension of life. My own hunch is that this hostility of tone is found more in the over-thirties (who may have old scores to settle) than among the younger generation. Concerning the young these words of a Spanish commentator seem more accurate:

> [At] 'the present moment the question of God remains something irrelevant, or even non-existent for the great majority of people. God is missing but is not missed. This is a genuinely new situation, which never existed before in the world'.[2]

Where this is true, unbelief has become an inherited confusion, a distance from roots, an unaggressive puzzlement about religious practices and their language, before Church religion and its mediations. This cultural unbelief is no longer de Lubac's 'drama of atheistic humanism', but rather an undramatic limbo of disinterest and non-belonging. Moreover, this religious vacuum is part of a larger unease and uncertainty about values, about institutions, about the very possibility of finding liveable meanings. In short, this kind of unbelief is more passive than chosen, more drifting than militant, and the unbeliever is more a victim of an impoverished or confusing culture than a deliberate rejecter of anything.

Cultural diagnosis: types of unbelief

With this general background, there seem to be four main groupings of culturally-rooted unbelief: religious anaemia; secularist marginalisation; anchorless spirituality; and cultural desolation. I will comment briefly on the first three and give more attention to the fourth.

What I mean by 'religious anaemia' includes many versions of distance from traditional Christian roots, where the fault for the malnutrition lies in a lack of pastoral imagination in the evangelising or educating community or Church. There is not so much a generation gap as a credibility gap of language, and this can take at least three forms.

(a) The typical mediations or dominant languages of Church can be simply experienced as a foreign tongue. The discourse of evangelisation may assume the presence of preambles of attitude or disposition that can no longer be taken for granted but have to be created and awoken.

(b) The pre-modern practices of Church are often more alienating than pastorally formative: they can assume a tone of authority that no longer exists, can seem to be a religion of moralisms that cultivates guilt, or else of sacramentalising the unevangelised, which in this culture can easily degenerate into sadly superficial ritualism. If there are no grounds in experience for what is being celebrated, then in this culture of experience rather than of tradition, the sacraments can remain pastorally fruitless.

(c) Here also one can include the spectrum ranging from disappointment to a new kind of anger concerning Church responses on various issues – sexual scandals concerning clergy or religious, approaches to women in today's world and Church, and a general impression of condescending non-listening to human realities. Even where these perceptions are mistaken, they cause a slide towards distance and distrust.

In short, religious anaemia is produced when the receiver encounters only the conventional or complacent externals of an institution, and when the communicators of faith fail to imitate St Paul on the Areopagus, entering initially and respectfully into the culture of the receiver.

These credibility gaps concerning Church are all the more

damaging to faith itself when there has been, as in Ireland, a tendency to over-identify Church with faith – in the sense of interpreting and measuring faith almost exclusively in terms of obedience to Church practices rather than in terms of a more explicit and personal commitment to Christ. This is our version of James Fowler's theory that most Christians never reach a maturity of individual commitment in faith, remaining instead at his 'stage 3' of institutional loyalty with all its risks of fragile dependence and of being easily shaken by the pressures of a dominant culture.

Turning to 'secular marginalisation': during a Plenary Assembly of the Pontifical Council for Culture in 1994, more than one speaker noted a new fear that the faith dimension cannot easily make itself heard in any public debate today and that there is a growing tendency to equate democracy with secular liberalism. Especially in the academic and media worlds, a secular culture reigns with the result that religion is subtly ignored as unimportant. One concrete example: having now lived in Italy for six years, I am struck by the contrast with Ireland in terms of serious newspaper attention to religion. In Italy even 'left-wing' or 'liberal' papers carry regular reviews of theological books. My impression is that this remains rare in Ireland and that a religious book is likely to be given a newspaper review only if it contains some element of controversy.

If 'anaemia' can be caused by an arrogance of authority, 'secular marginalisation' seems to involve an arrogance of autonomy, a somewhat adolescent rebellion against what the middle-aged once knew as religion. Culturally this marginalisation causes a collapse of 'plausibility structures' (Peter Berger), whereby a whole range of interpretation of life comes to appear unreal, or as unworthy 'baby food'. In short, this is a form of unbelief through silence and shyness in the fields of reflection and communication.

What I am calling 'anchorless spirituality' points in an

opposite direction and is one of the surprises of post-modernity – the so-called return of the sacred. When people find themselves 'sated but unsatisfied' by the old materialism, as well as bored or untouched by their experience of Church, they can enter a new search without anchors. It is that drifting that constitutes a danger: the hunger is good but, in so far as secular culture weakens people's Christian roots, such a spiritual trend leaves itself open to becoming a mixture of ancient heresies like gnosticism and pelagianism.

In a context of religious malnutrition, such lonely spirituality easily becomes another form of dechristianisation. Without community and contemplation, it risks being a narcissism without Christ. In other words, this phenomenon is a product of the two elements already described: where Church discourse fails to connect with human needs and where culture gradually forces religious consciousness into the realm of the private, then fundamental spiritual hungers in people become lonely and yet desperate in their search for some kind of food. Thrown back on their own resources, people express their undernourished and suppressed religiousness in different ways which can range, depending largely on temperament, from so-called New Age explorations to more fundamentalist rigidities.[3]

My fourth diagnostic is one of 'cultural desolation', and the keywords here will be disposition, imagination and freedom. In brief I want to argue that the pressures of the dominant culture leave many people blocked in a cultural desolation on the level of disposition or readiness for faith. Why? Because these pressures kidnap their imagination in trivial ways and therefore leave them unfree for Revelation. Or, more precisely, for the hearing from which faith comes (as St Paul says in Romans 10).

Some people bemoan the fact that schools or parishes are not teaching people the catechism any more, and that young people leave their education with little clear notion of the meaning of Christian faith or Church worship. The point is valid, but I am not convinced by the emphasis on an exclusively conceptual version of truth. I would insist more on the impact of a certain cultural conditioning on the level of freedom of disposition rather than doctrine. Hence a first task in this situation is a ministry of disposition, an awakening of the hungers to which the truth may eventually be seen as answer. In this spirit William Barry warns that the 'influence of culture on us escapes our consciousness' and that we need to find out 'how any of us encultured human beings can become free enough from our culture to be believers'.[4]

If the main faith blockages today come from cultural desolation on the level of disposition or readiness for faith, how can people move towards that consolation or openness where faith can be born? It will mean liberating levels of hearing and of desire that become stifled in the everyday culture. But before the positive liberation of wonder, perhaps there is a need for a certain negative clearing of the ground. Education is invited to become counter-cultural, in the sense of helping students to identify the dehumanising factors present in life-styles and assumptions of the culture. In today's situation a main task and challenge for religious education is about how faith-choices can be made both within and against a culture. To survive as believers into the twenty-first century, young people will need to develop skills of Christian critique and of seeing through the deceptions of the surrounding culture. Indeed, to be a Christian, even today, means opting for a certain resistance movement, distancing oneself from the diminished life on offer in the dominant images around. But we need a note of caution here about the tone of our judgments. Too often we can fall into mere moaning about 'isms' (materialism, hedonism, immanentism...). Christian critique is not generalised moaning. Discernment is concrete and ultimately positive – in search of genuine life.

It is worth recalling that Cardinal Newman always insisted that unbelief arises not from the intellect but from the state of one's heart, and that the crucial battle zone for faith or unbelief lies in the imagination. In his *Grammar of Assent* he wrote: 'the heart is commonly reached not through the reason, but through the imagination', adding, with typical understatement, 'no man will be a martyr for a conclusion'.[5] As a similar comment on modern culture I have often quoted a statement made some fifty years ago by the poet, T. S. Eliot: 'The trouble of the modern age is not merely the inability to believe certain things about God which our forefathers believed, but the inability to feel towards God and man as they did'.[6] This locates the crisis not in creeds but in sensibility or imagination; it suggests that we have not so much a crisis of faith in the sense of a crisis of creed or message, as a crisis in the *language* or mediations of faith.

In this light my thesis about cultural desolation and a resultant lack of freedom for faith locates itself more definitely in the worlds of imagination and sensibility. The secular rhythms of culture can lure the human imagination into an incapacity for genuine attention to the call of God. Or again the cultural messages embodied in the images around us enter the imagination unnoticed and become assumptions about reality that cause what Buber called an 'eclipse of God'. On both levels the disposition or desire for faith becomes stifled through cultural desolation.

Towards discernment and cultural agency
It is relatively easy to identify conflict between faith and culture on the level of values and vision – seeing how a market-dominated culture promotes short-term everything for the competing and consuming self, leaving little room for commitments, reconciliation, self-giving, and other Christian expressions of faith. But the real desolation is deeper. The culture in the driving seat of our imaginations and attitudes can erode not so much these lived embodiments of faith as the very possibility of faithing at all. The battle is not only over specific

issues like sexual fidelity or consumerism or competitive uncaring. They are symptoms of a more fundamental clash of visions. The primary battle is that faith itself as a covenant gift, a yes to a yes, can be rendered unreal for vast numbers of young people who have few skills for seeing through the deceptions of the culture. How can education provide shields against this kidnapping of their spiritual imagination? By teaching the basics of an aggressive discernment of the surrounding culture and by offering them the building bricks not only of mature faith but of cultural agency.

In his recent study, *Critique of Modernity,* Alain Touraine is under no illusion about the 'charms of the self' exercised by the propaganda of what he calls the 'programmed' liberal system of society; if they win, the result is a stunted person, sucked into 'deceptive individualist consumerism', and incapable of reaching the level of being an 'actor', with a 'capacity for consciousness and resistance'.[7] Such a victory of conformism over agency is deeply dehumanising: to translate Touraine into an image, it is like one of those programmed lifts in a twenty-storey skyscraper than only stop between the third and sixth floors. Hence most of the range of one's humanity remains untouched, unvisited, uninvited into life. The non-actor is the one who unconsciously follows the life agenda, the limiting culture of the system.

Indeed we can elaborate metaphor even further: Christian education is a matter of developing acting schools, preparing people for agency within the theatre of contemporary culture. What might be the curriculum in such an academy? Like any acting school it would involve training in certain skills and disciplines, skills of awareness concerning personal potentials and alertness about cultural realities. Again, like any acting school, it would require group work, a sense of ensemble and of belonging with one another. It would seek to bring out people's capacity to express experience; in short it would liberate their human languages to create a character and a world. Finally, any acting school has to form people's sensibility to know the depths of human suffering that are often hidden. Acting in this sense is subversive: it wants to incarnate what is easily suppressed.

Even 'coming to see that one has a way of seeing involves a shift in consciousness'.[8] As a first step towards a Christian option of life, education would help people identify the commodity philosophy (a form of lived atheism) that the dominant culture both assumes and promotes: only then can one come to recognise inevitable 'oppositions between cultural wisdom and Christian wisdom'.[9] This awakening to a possible tyranny of images is only an initial stage in any cultural discernment. Awareness alone is insufficient: unless the Christian community becomes a producer of meaning, its discernment will remain passive. As Pope John Paul II said, challengingly, in his letter of foundation for the Pontifical Council of Culture: 'A faith that does not become culture is . . . not fully lived out'.[10]

The same insight is developed by one commentator on 'cultural agency' who claims that 'a religious culture of resistance is impossible unless it is grounded in patterned ways of living that embody an alternative vision of life'.[11] In other words cultural discernment has two phases, one of interpretation and judgement, and the other of communal spirituality and creation of Christian life structures. Without constant self-critique the Church can 'become too comfortable with Caesar' instead of subverting the domination of the 'commodity kingdom': 'If the Christian does feel at home, something is drastically wrong'.[12]

An obvious battleground here involves the relation between the official faith-vision of the school and the unofficial cultural agenda lived in the daily praxis of both school and society. In practice it can be a zone of ambiguity, where the Christian ideals of the institution are subtly undermined by the pressures of competition (from examinations to sport) or from the alternative curriculum of liberal relativism and self-fulfilment that is so easily absorbed from the wider culture – including of course the culture of the parents. In order to make sense within the implied norms of the dominant culture, even religious formation can fall into what Michael Warren calls a 'Jesus reduction program', offering a soft picture of Christ that 'neatly fits the aspirations of middle-class' culture.[13]

Conclusion: disconnected from depth

I have been arguing that unbelief today is often grounded in a culturally conditioned lack of spiritual freedom and that the main blockages to faith are not intellectual but on the level of imagination. Education in the sense of schooling cannot be expected to confront and respond to this challenge on its own but it has a major role to play which will involve a shifting of its own vision of priorities. Above all some adapted version of cultural study and cultural discernment seems crucial for religious eduction today. It would help students to reflect on the lights and shadows of their major, if hidden, curriculum of values and vision. Above all it would seek to counter the basic danger that the culture fosters an inability to reach those levels of humanity where hunger and hearing can be experienced. Because faith stems from both, it needs a spirit of search but also a receptivity for the Word. If the superficialities of culture induce a communal disconnection from depth, education needs to reconnect people to those layers of listening where wisdom can be glimpsed.[14]

The lived culture can seem merely a source of drift, but that is never the whole story: the whole zone of culture is inevitably the place where meanings are formed, consciously or unconsciously, and as such it is more than merely a source of the numbing of religious sensibility that I have called cultural unbelief. The Canadian philosopher, Charles Taylor, warns against mere pessimism about the ills of modernity. Behind even the trivial expressions one can recognise genuine ideals of authentic living. In order to confront a sense of impotence he proposes a kind of communal discernment: 'the mechanisms of inevitability work only when people are divided and fragmented. The predicament alters when there comes to be a common consciousness. We don't want to exaggerate our degrees of freedom. But they are not zero'.[15]

A merely cultural faith is weak in the sense of being over-dependent on social supports. But a non-cultural faith is not the answer: it would be condemned to privacy and impotence. Faith needs to find its cultural voice in the sense of having the wisdom to recognise the deep and positive values emerging within culture, as well as the discernment to critique and even heal the dehumanising wounds present in every human culture. A faith that seeks to become culture means that the faith community seeks to express its treasure, non-arrogantly and serenely, within the circles of searching that constitute conscious culture.

Today we see much more clearly than before that we are both shaped by and shapers of the contexts of our self-understandings. If we are only shaped by these emerging contexts, then we become merely passive members of a dominant culture: we assimilate whatever values and disvalues happen to come along. But if we can awaken to this shaping ocean called culture, within which we swim, then we stop being potential victims and move towards being possible agents of culture. We emerge from drifting and make some decisions. But between passivity and agency, there is a crucial intermediate step of discernment and critique. We choose with more clear-sighted freedom what deserves a yes and what a no in the supermarket of lived culture, or among the clashing symbols of the more creative culture.[16] In the complicated debate about the role of religion in education now, I feel privileged to have had this first word, and to say, very simply, that what I have been calling cultural consciousness will surely have a central role in any education, secular or religious, but that within a religious horizon it is part of the healing of culturally-induced blockage to faith and, indeed, a road to a more mature faith, more worthy of the moment of cultural upheaval we are already living.

3

THE PLACE OF THEOLOGY AND RELIGION IN HIGHER EDUCATION

Michael Drumm

At first sight a topic like the one I have been asked to address might appear quaint and almost opaque. Surely in the real world of academic striving, with its emphases on rigorous research, exact empirical observation and openness to ideas and the imagination, religion and theology appear as little more than medieval concerns of interest purely to the historian of ideas. After all what can one research? What is to be observed? Are there any new ideas? Is the imagination not suppressed? This paper will seek to address these questions from the perspective of a working Catholic theologian in the Irish context, particularly the constitutional and institutional context of the Republic of Ireland.

What then is a theologian? Not, certainly, an expert on God. Could you think of a more obscene notion, than to circumscribe the divine in our little academic pursuit? Good theology never did that, bad theology always does. In fact, theology at its best is a pretty agnostic affair; two great theologians, Thomas Aquinas (1225-74) and Karl Rahner (1904-84), came to very agnostic conclusions towards the end of their lives.[1] God is the one who, when known, is unknown. God is not the answer to all human problems but the question of freedom and finitude which will never go away. As a theologian I try to wander around the sacred spaces in the world and in the soul, to visit the corners of brokenness and emptiness and yet hear the call to transcendence, to hope against hope and, in a very traditional language, to know the depth of my own sinfulness and the breadth of divine love. I would like to apologise to you for all the cheap theological answers you've heard to life's most heart-rending questions. I would like to apologise for the horrible burden of fear and self-doubt sown over centuries by theologians and preachers. But even as we acknowledge past failures we must be careful not to dismiss religious sensibilities as little more than personal whim or social conformism. The academic study of theology should help to deepen our reflections on the very nature of religious experience.

For most Irish people theology is a strange study. Recently I heard two interesting uses of the word 'theological'. The London correspondent of *The Irish Times* remarked that his predictions on the nature of elections to an assembly in Northern Ireland were touching on a 'heavily theological area'. A criminologist, when asked about his opinion on reform of bail laws, commented that he didn't take a 'theological approach' to such issues: the laws were not written on tablets of stone and so they could be changed! When students who are following courses in theology or religious studies at third level are asked by their peers 'and what are you studying?' their response is greeted with incredulity. Unquestionably some of these attitudes flow from the traditional Irish mistrust of ideas and suspicion of intellectuals, but the association of rigorous thought with religious belief appears particularly problematical to the Irish psyche.

Voices such as the Bishop of Cork and Ross,[2] an editorial in *The Irish Times*[3] and the President of St Patrick's College, Maynooth,[4] have recently called for the full acceptance of the discipline of theology in institutions of higher education in the Republic of Ireland. By this I presume they mean the acceptance and funding of theology by the State in the same manner as other areas of study and not the establishment of actual third-level institutions, a large number of which already exist and thrive. Given that the State has no difficulty in funding the teaching of religion at first and second level it seems strange that theology should be treated differently from all other disciplines at third level. Some, coming from a libertarian perspective, will object on philosophical grounds that religious belief is at best a purely personal affair or at worst a pernicious illusion which cannot be subjected to proper scientific rigour. As a result it should be excluded from the academy. I would like to argue against such an approach and even go so far as to suggest that the full incorporation of theology as an integral element in third-level education will enrich the academy and demonstrate the maturity of our civic structures.

One of the world's leading theologians, David Tracy, speaks of theology having three publics: the academy, the Church and society.[5] Unfortunately in Ireland it has spoken to only one such public – the Church. And traditionally this public discourse has been dominated too much by the Reformation context, to such an extent that as late as the 1950s we find the leading minds of the Irish Catholic Church studying questions such as attendance of Catholics at non-Catholic weddings, the right of lay sacristans to touch sacred vessels, whether Catholic support of functions in aid of Protestant Churches is licit, and many other issues in the same vein.[6] Given this mind-set it is not surprising that Vatican II (1962-65) came as such a surprise to the Irish Churches; elsewhere in Europe the ground had been prepared through theological reflection and publications but in Ireland it was only after the Council that creative minds began to give us new language and new insights. A great debt of gratitude is owed to these post-Vatican II theologians and it is on the basis of the foundations that they have laid that we can now analyse the relationship of theology to the Irish academy, Irish society and the Irish Churches.

Theology and the Irish academy

Religion and theology are very important in higher and

continuing education because they help to overcome the error of perceiving religion as something you grow out of; this is suggested by its traditional absence from third-level institutions. This suggests that religion does not really stand up to academic analysis, that it is only suited to endless meandering debates on radio and television. The reality is that there are few areas in more need of research and reflection than religious belief.

In Irish higher education the question of the place of theology is not a new one. From the Reformation onwards issues concerning theological education have plagued Ireland. These controversies led to the establishment of the Irish Colleges in Rome, Paris, Salamanca, Louvain etc. Ever since the 1840s the place of theology in the university in Ireland has caused great difficulties, mainly because of the complete dominance of the Reformation context. Relations between Catholics and Protestants in Ireland underwent fractious deterioration in the first half of the nineteenth century with a new proselytising zeal on the part of many Anglicans and the first real application of the structures and disciplines of the Tridentine Counter-Reformation to Irish Catholicism. On no issue did divisions focus so clearly as on education and, even more precisely, on university education.[7] Over many decades the Queens' Colleges, the Catholic University and the National University dealt with theology in very different ways. Given the ferocity of the debates in the nineteenth century it was not surprising that it was decided to set the teaching of theology to one side in the establishment of the National University. The 1908 Act which established the National University of Ireland made it illegal for the State to fund the teaching of theology. A professor could be appointed but only on the basis of private benefaction. As a result of the 1908 Act and the inclusion of the clause that the State will 'not endow any religion' in the 1920 Government of Ireland Act and in Bunreacht na hEireann (Article 44.2.2), the ironic situation emerged that the Republic of Ireland is the only member of the European Union where theology is not publicly funded at third level.[8] Michael Nolan comments:

> The phrase 'endow a religion' has a long history in Westminster legislation affecting Ireland. Before its use in the Government of Ireland Act of 1920, it is found in the Government of Ireland Bill of 1914 and in the Home Rule Bills of 1893 and 1886. The concern of the Westminster parliament with this issue can be traced back to the Irish Church Act of 1869, which disestablished and disendowed the Church of Ireland ... Having reluctantly agreed to the disendowing of the Church of Ireland, the Westminster parliament was adamant, whenever a bill came up to give devolved government ('Home Rule') to Ireland, that no Irish parliament should have the power to establish or endow another Church.[9]

It's interesting to note that the Republic of Ireland has interpreted the non-endowment of theology at third level rather differently than the State in Northern Ireland. In Northern Ireland it has been interpreted as referring to the ethics of legislation, that one should not endow one religion to the exclusion of another, whereas in the Republic it has been interpreted as a constitutional impediment.[10]

As a result of this the provision of theology courses, diplomas and degrees at third level in the Republic of Ireland has evolved in a very haphazard way throughout the twentieth century. Today there is a large number of institutions offering third-level qualifications of one sort or another in theology, catechetics, religious education and religious studies. Some of the institutions involved are: Pontifical University, Maynooth; Milltown Institute of Theology and Philosophy, Dublin; Trinity College, Dublin; Mater Dei Institute of Education, Dublin; Church of Ireland Theological College, Dublin; Irish School of Ecumenics,

Dublin; St Patrick's College, Dublin; St Catherine's College, Dublin; Holy Cross College, Dublin; All Hallows Institute, Dublin; Kimmage Mission Institute, Dublin; St Mary's Dominican House of Studies, Dublin; University College, Dublin; Mary Immaculate College, Limerick; St Angela's College, Sligo; St Peter's College, Wexford; St John's College, Waterford; St Patrick's College, Carlow; St Patrick's College, Thurles; University College, Cork; Regional Technical College, Galway.[11] A few points come immediately to mind: firstly, the geographical dominance of Dublin (though of course this only mirrors the same reality in all aspects of life in the Irish Republic); secondly, whilst small can indeed be beautiful questions must be raised about the academic and financial viability of so many small institutions in terms of the quality of teaching personnel, academic research and publications, library and other resources. We can only hope that the future development of theology as an academic discipline is coordinated in such a way that standards are protected and the quality of the provision enhanced. In the longer run only proper public funding can guarantee these standards.

Public funding is currently provided to a very limited extent but with interesting strings attached, the most interesting being that the State seems to have difficulties with the very term 'theology'. This is important as it raises questions already faced in other countries. Theology can and should be contrasted with comparative religious studies; the latter has for its focus what all religions have in common, i.e. it follows a phenomenological approach prescinding from questions of truth and personal faith. The danger is that it amounts to little more than analysis of the lowest common denominator which all religions share. Theology can include a component element of comparative religious studies but it must go well beyond the limitations of a comparative framework as it deals with issues such as the nature of personal faith, the claims made on human living by belief in a personal God, how the call to self-transcendence might be facilitated in a particular ecclesial setting. Theology is not primarily concerned with the phenomenon of religion in general but with the truth claims of a particular tradition.

Does this mean that theology is condemned to be a sectarian enterprise? If the answer is 'yes' then clearly the State could not fund theology faculties. It might try to find a way around this by funding only multi-denominational theology, but then the question arises about what exactly this is. In reality there is no such thing; what exists are different forms of denominational theology as each theologian comes from a particular tradition. Of course a department of inter-denominational theology could be conceived of and there is much to be said in favour of such a scenario. Yet the key fact would remain that the individual theologian comes from a particular tradition. Despite the fact that this appears to be a serious problem for theology in the academy I believe it is one of its strengths, pointing as it does to the hermeneutical nature of the discipline.

Contemporary theology is one of the most hermeneutically aware of all disciplines as a result of the revolution in biblical studies during this century. Modern biblical scholarship has awoken us to the historicity of the normative texts of the Christian tradition; it has contextualised these texts in the cultural worlds from which they emerged and it has revealed how the presuppositions of the reader can bring new meanings to the text. This process has alerted all serious theologians to the centrality of tradition – every text is a partial expression of a particular tradition and all readers come to a text with the insights and baggage of their own tradition and context.[12] Many insights have followed from this: there is not only one but several different theologies within the New Testament itself; all traditions are characterised by plurality and ambiguity, by insight and blindness; there is no such thing as a presuppositionless objectivist standpoint from where one can critique classical texts and tradition, one must always begin from where one is, which is always in the middle; there is no escaping from one's tradition but rather the challenge is to appropriate one's tradition authentically. Such a challenge is extraordinarily demanding as one must face the discontinuities, the fissures, the brokenness and the pain in the pluralities and the ambiguities of one's tradition and one's own life. One of the key functions of the theologian is to establish criteria to facilitate the authentic appropriation of one's tradition. A crucial criterion that has emerged in the work of many theologians is encounter with the 'other', with the otherness of different Christian denominations, the otherness of the great world religions, the otherness of atheism and unbelief, the otherness of poverty and social exclusion. These varied insights have already led to enormous change and creative endeavour manifest in fields as diverse as catechetics,[13] cinema[14] and pastoral planning.[15] All important developments in religious consciousness have been premised on advances in theology.

Based on these varied perspectives and notwithstanding all the historical problems, I believe that theology should take its place alongside other disciplines in the Irish academy. Nobody would suggest that history or philosophy should be excluded from the civil academy even though the work of historians and philosophers is obviously informed by (maybe even predetermined by) the social, political and cultural context into which one is born and the life experience (for better or worse) of the individual thinker. The easy claims to objectivity so characteristic of many academics involved in the human sciences are not so obvious as might at first appear. Objectivity is not just a matter of taking a detached look at things but the slow process of attempting to express one's own subjectivity authentically and self-critically. Bias, tradition and context are part of what we all are; only through a self-critical analysis can we appropriate these realities anew and foster an authentic expression of human subjectivity. The theologian can perform just such a self-critical analysis of religion, which is clearly one of the most important aspects of Irish society.

Theology and Irish society

Given the significance of religion in Irish society and history one would imagine that there are few more fertile areas than theology for academic research and reflection. But in its preoccupation with the polemics of Catholic/Protestant relationships theology has contributed little to Irish society. Over the last twenty years theologians have begun to break out of the Reformation strait-jacket and to engage new 'dialogue partners', foremost amongst which has been secular humanism as a mature expression of an atheistic world-view. But there is a whole other range of possible 'dialogue partners' – traditions and forces which are significant in Irish society and history and with which Irish theologians must surely engage. Amongst them might be included popular religiosity, militant republicanism, Celtic tradition, missionary outreach, emigration, rural decline, social exclusion, sexual revolution. Only through dialogue with these various realities can theology develop a properly public language.[16]

The failure to engage fully in public discourse in the academy and in society in general has seriously impoverished both theology as an academic discipline and the quality of public debates on sensitive social issues. Such debates tend to be characterised on the one hand by Catholic fundamentalism, epitomised by Judge Rory O'Hanlon with his theocratic arguments in the recent divorce referendum; and on the other by an insufferable dismissal by the liberal intelligentia of religious sensibilities, as amounting to nothing more than personal sentimentality. The task of theology is not to mediate between these extremes but to provide a public language which would enable all of us to engage in a public discourse, laying bare the various presuppositions at work and demonstrating that there is no presuppositionless perspective. Engaging in such public discourse is the key role of the theologian; failure to do so leaves the theologian open to the charge of being involved in a privatised gnosticism. This is the classic failure of theology – it becomes opaque and quaint, indeed downright boring and irrelevant. But the task is far from easy; theology must bring the most radical personal reflection into the public domain as the theologian attempts 'in fidelity to a profoundly personal but not private vision, to find the skills to speak publicly again'.[17] It is interesting to note that on a recent visit to Ireland the Czech President Vaclav Havel spoke of the need for a political discourse that embraced conscience and responsibility, infinity and the transcendent, the mystery of the world and the order of being. However, he acknowledged that it was difficult to engage those who form opinion with such ideas, for it is 'as if such thoughts were to them largely a matter of a private whim or personal hobby that does not belong on the public scene of politics.'[18] It is the task of theology in its conversation with the public of the academy and of society to foster an ambience that is open to such sensibilities.

Unfortunately issues of control and power have dominated all major debates that involve religion to such an extent that the excellent work done by some theologians has been sidelined. This is all the more regrettable given the insights their research could bring to bear on important issues such as Church/State relations, Catholic /Protestant difficulties, a Christian vision of the future, the historical failures of the Churches, the Irish contribution to Catholicism internationally etc. The preoccupation with issues of law and control is particularly evident in debates concerning education. If one analyses the Green Paper and the White Paper on education one could only be struck by the paucity of material relating to religion; at the National Education Convention issues of law and management dominated with regard to the role of religion. The only form of public discourse we seem to use in regard to religion/education issues concerns power and control. Understandably this antagonises many people and suggests that most of the key decisions are made behind the scenes. We must move beyond a language created in the polemical atmosphere of the nineteenth century. Theology and theologians can contribute to a new form of discourse but in the process of doing so I believe two realities need to be acknowledged: the State must accept and applaud the overwhelming historical contribution of the Churches to Irish education and the Churches must apologise for the wrongs done to some wonderful educationalists who were sidelined or in some cases dismissed simply because they did not measure up to very limited notions of orthodoxy. The healing of institutional relationships could be an important theological goal.

Theology and the Irish Churches

Whatever about its interaction with the public of society, theology has often spoken to the public of the Irish Churches but in a language that meant it was seldom if ever heard. The function of theology was little more than a passport to ordination; few pastors found it to be what it should have been – an endless source of enlightenment and creative insight for pastoral practice and preaching. Instead it appeared linguistically distant and elitist with little to say to the ordinary believer. Not nearly enough attention was paid to pedagogy. This was an outstanding failure, given that the ecclesial function of theology is surely to help believers articulate and understand their faith and tradition, to be able (in the famous words of St Peter's first epistle) to give the reason for the hope which is in you (1 Peter 3:15). Theologians must bear responsibility for the level of theological illiteracy which is manifest in Ireland although this is also due to the anti-intellectual trait so characteristic of Irish Catholicism. One way or another things are now beginning to change and the two great signs of change are to be found in adult religious education and the laicisation of theology in general.

Over the last twenty years many developments have occurred in adult religious education. The overall experience for participants has been truly liberating. When religious consciousness is subjected to critical but sympathetic analysis people can discover new dimensions and indeed worlds of meaning that they barely knew existed. There is no doubt in my mind, based on my own experience of adult religious education, of the pedagogical significance of theology in fostering a more mature faith. The future of the Church in Ireland is intimately linked with adult religious education. We are entering an era in the western world where large numbers of people will have received a relatively good general education. Many will have received an excellent education in their chosen field. A simplistic and sometimes superstitious approach to faith will not satisfy these people. If we continue to feed them only on the staple diet of Sunday homilies, preaching that they must live out on weekdays what they proclaim on Sundays without giving them the power or insight to do so, then it is as if we are giving stones to those asking for bread. People respond to a good diet of biblical study and pastorally aware theology. What is most striking in Ireland today is the number of people who find traditional religious answers insufficient for the world in which they live. Consequently they turn to new spiritualities, eastern religions and even the occult in search of a liberating message. But can theology really be liberating? Initially the study of theology can be deeply disturbing but this is not surprising in a country like Ireland where many people, even those in very advanced positions in their own careers, cling to a childlike expression of faith. We must face the fact that when these people are introduced to new ideas and horizons of religious faith they become uncomfortable with the status quo in terms of ideas, language and structures. The journey of faith has opened up anew for them. This raises important questions for bishops, preachers and teachers.

Traditionally the only locus for theology was the seminary. That day is now happily past. The vast majority of those now following theology courses in colleges and adult groups do so out of personal interest – either to deepen their knowledge of the particular area or to embark upon a career in an educational or ecclesial setting. The clericalisation of theology is coming rapidly to an end. This raises important questions for the Churches, the academy and society. For the Churches, the laicisation of theology will, in the medium term, become the key to renewal. In the meantime it will probably lead to a lot of argument and disagreement. The biggest problem at the moment is the frustration found among many lay people who have received theological qualifications, for although theology has become laicised, most full-time paid employment in the Churches is still dominated by ordained clergy. For the academy, it takes theology beyond the realm of the seminary and means that the subject can no longer be dismissed as little more than a necessity for ordination. For society in general, it offers the possibility of developing a new language for understanding what religion is. Nobody should underestimate the revolution that is involved in the laicisation of theology; lay believers will express and reflect upon Christian faith in new and exciting ways; the ecclesial future is not nearly so bleak as some people imagine.

For the Irish Catholic Church there are particular questions that theological renewal will raise. The religious tradition of Irish Catholicism must face the critique of modern reason. Modernity has come of age in Ireland. The coincidence of Vatican II with industrialisation in the Republic of Ireland in the 1960s is remarkable. As a result the changes in the social, economic and ecclesial worlds have been overwhelming over the last thirty years. The icons of religious authority – persons, structures and texts, are daily under question. The great tragedy is that loyal adherents might retreat into a ghetto where iconophile consciousness can supposedly survive untarnished. The iconoclasm of modernity is deeply offensive and alienating to many Catholics. There is much in the modernist critique of religion that is adolescent and reductionist but a fatal response would be to withdraw into the world of the village, cosily secure in our own certainties but utterly incapable of interacting with the world of modernity. Theology will enable believers to dialogue with those who sincerely disagree with them, to challenge the values of modernity, to articulate their faith in such a way that those who belittle it will be seen to be the narrow-minded people, to speak a word of faith and hope in the midst of the world's nihilism and despair. The Irish Catholic Church owes its members no less than this.

There is one last important question from a Catholic standpoint and that is the relationship between the Magisterium of the Catholic Church and the theologian. The two have different roles: the members of the Magisterium are the bishops of the Church who are duty-bound to teach and hand on the doctrine of the faith in ever-changing circumstances; theologians are asked to serve the Church, including the Magisterium, through reflecting on the meaning of Christian faith, raising new questions, facing new challenges, articulating possible new horizons, pointing out past failures.[19] At times there will obviously be tension between these two crucial realities in the life of the Church but for the believer the two exist on completely different levels – one is not asked to have faith in the work of a theologian whereas one is asked to have faith in the doctrine of the Church as taught by the Magisterium. The Magisterium then clearly has primacy in the life of the Catholic Church but in its teaching it should pay close attention to the work of theologians who, understandably, are moving onwards to new frontiers in their efforts to read the signs of the times.

Conclusion

Historically theology can justly be accused of seriously inhibiting the development of the natural sciences. As far as many historians of ideas are concerned the Dark Ages were dark precisely because of theological obscurantism. At its worst theology was and still remains one of the most ideologically objectionable of all human endeavours but at its best it was and still can be liberating, humane, insightful and radically critical of unjust structures. Anyone who underestimates the power of the Christian Gospel to foster commitment is foolish. Anyone who completely rejects the value of religion in human striving is deaf to much that is wonderful in the human spirit. Anyone who is blind to the dangers of religious zealotry is blind to the facts of history. All of this points to the need for serious theological reflection.

But such reflection is not an easy task. There is a very important question concerning the proper locus of theological endeavour; is it the university, the parish, the interest group, the marginalised (as suggested by liberation theology)? Whatever way that question is answered, we should not doubt that in order to speak a word of faith and hope to our contemporaries, theologians must revisit the margins of their own experience and the margins of their society; only there will they find the language and the courage necessary for the task. It is particularly apposite to end my reflections by reference to John Henry Newman, one of the great theologians of all time who attempted to establish a university in Dublin where theology would have taken its place alongside all the other disciplines. Newman wrote:

> Perhaps the reason why the standard of holiness among us is so low, why our attainments are so poor, our view of the truth so dim, our belief so unreal, our general notions so artificial and external is this, that we dare not trust each other with the secret of our hearts.... We do not probe the wounds of our nature thoroughly; we do not lay the foundation of our religious profession in the ground of our

inner man; we make clean the outside of things; we are amiable and friendly to each other in words and deeds, but our love is not enlarged, our bowels of affection are straitened, and we fear to let the intercourse begin at the root; and, in consequence, our religion, viewed as a social system, is hollow. The presence of Christ is not in it.[20]

Theology is asked to reflect upon and speak of these things in a way that can be heard in the academy, in society and in the particular Churches. Let's hope, for all our sakes, that theology is at its best in the Ireland of the future.

FIRST DISCUSSION

Chair: Dr Geraldine Smyth OP
Panel: Dr Michael Paul Gallagher SJ
Rev Michael Drumm

Geraldine Smyth: The floor is open and you are free to address your questions to either of the speakers.

Roddy Day, primary teacher: I'd like to thank both speakers for two great papers. I'd like to ask a very direct question to both: Can you teach religion and not believe in it? Or could you lecture in theology and not believe in it? For instance, couldn't you as a teacher simply be challenged by the notion that children have to learn some prayers, or, at third level, be challenged by theology as an intellectual discipline. There are teachers who are attempting to teach religion at present and they don't believe in it.

Geraldine Smyth: We'll take another question before asking our speakers to respond.

Professor John Coolahan: I'd also like to thank both speakers for very illuminating papers, with a spirit and vision behind them which is rare, but very welcome in the arena of religion in Irish education. And this is where my question comes in. Part of the historical difficulties that arose in relation to the acceptance of theology, and State support for theology was linked, in the pre-independence period, with the very strong and unequivocal statements of the episcopacy that if theology was to be taught in the university, it had to be in accordance with the episcopacy's view of what the nature of that theology would be. To a very large degree this view was that theology should be an exposition of the Magisterium, rather than the tradition of open enquiry and exploring, letting the search of truth follow where it may, with the clash of ideas and symbols which is part of that search. Really, this view of theology was held right through the decades after independence as well. It may be changing now. We'll just have to wait and see whether it is or not. A great deal depends on the kinds of attitudes which both of you exemplified this evening. The richness of your presentations has not been common in public debate about theology in Ireland. Very many lay people believe that we have suffered badly by not having theology in the university. But the causes and the contextual factors are crucial and we need to get it right.

The same holds true about much of the current debate on educational reform. I don't quite agree for instance, that the National Education Convention dealt only with control issues. It dealt with a whole load of things. But the main reason why much of public debate on education policy doesn't go into the area of religion and comment on it, is that right down along the line we were told that the Church will deal with the religious issues, that programmes in religion are the business of the Churches. Far from being encouraged to comment, lay people were positively discouraged from commenting. They were frequently afraid to do so, because any slips or mistakes – albeit ones made in good faith – would invoke public censure from ecclesiastical authority. That has been an important reason why so few lay people entered the debate about religion and theology in education, at least in a public way. Whether we can change this tradition and open things out a bit more I don't know, but I hope we can. In any case there are some crucial issues here.

Geraldine Smyth: Michael Paul Gallagher, would you like to comment on the first question here? And perhaps Michael Drumm can open the response on the second.

Michael Paul Gallagher: In replying to the first question maybe I could start by drawing on the distinction Michael Drumm made between theology and religious studies. I think I could be a professor of religious studies without being a believer. But I couldn't be a theologian and not be a believer. However, I'll give one brief example from the school situation. I have a good friend who is a teacher and he calls himself an unbeliever. He goes to Mass because of the children and that's about it. And we have had many good discussions. He tells me that he loves teaching religion. Why? 'Because', he declares, 'at primary level the books are so good'. He says 'I follow the books with imagination, perhaps one day I'll believe it'. So, that's my footnote to that question.

Geraldine Smyth: Would you like to take the second question?

Michael Paul Gallagher: Yes, I resonate with what you [John Coolahan] are saying. I would think that all of that talk of control and being afraid to get things wrong, and getting frowned on from on high is simply pre-modernity: the village world. It is gone, and gone for good. It may still have some few backlashes, but nobody will pay too much attention. If we are in anything like modernity, or post-modernity, and I believe we are in both – indeed moving rapidly from one into the other – we are in a time when the majority of theologians will be lay theologians, where the clerical professional will no longer be the typical theologian. And the lay theologian will have a completely different sensibility – for instance, a woman theologian, with a different sensibility for alternative aspects of theology, and less worry about getting things 'correct' and so on. So I think history is inviting us into a new agenda. To stick with the old agenda is just nostalgia.

Michael Drumm: I agree with all that Michael Paul Gallagher has said so there is no point in my repeating it. Just briefly, then, let me give another perspective on the first question. It is one of the great theological questions of our time: Can you be a theologian and not believe it? and, at a different level, could you teach religion and not believe it? As Michael Paul Gallagher suggests, the general perspective is to draw a distinction between comparative religious studies – where people explore and comment on the phenomenon of religion, and on the other hand, theology, where people deal with real faith questions and here some kind of real faith would be suggested, even if an implicit one. I must confess however that in my theological experience, everybody has some kind of implicit belief, though it mightn't be an institutionalised kind of religious belief. And this is a great crux where teachers at primary level in Irish schools are concerned: people are forced to teach religion simply because they teach in a particular kind of school. There is no doubt that in the longer run this is a problem that simply has to be addressed, because people will object on all sorts of grounds and their objections are perfectly understandable from a theological point of view, not to mention the point of view of secular humanism. I think that theologically, I'd like to say that you can teach theology, and you can teach religion, even though you are not a believer in the ordinary sense of the word. In my view, there are very few complete non-believers. There are large numbers who don't believe in the institutional Church, but there are very few who don't believe in the transcendental side of life. And, in all fairness, that's where the primary programme, and indeed the second-level programme in religion, would like to direct people.

To respond to the second question, I don't want to criticise the National Education Convention, except on one very precise issue, which is actually a Church issue. I only meant that where religious representatives and people from other sectors of education were discussing things with each other, the discussion focused too narrowly on matters like law and control. Otherwise

I don't want to criticise or in any way to take from what was a very historic event in Irish education. But John Coolahan is quite right to put his finger on how the self-understanding of Irish Catholics relates to the question of the relationship between the episcopacy, which is the Magisterium, and the theologian. That is the most controversial question in post-Conciliar Catholicism, i.e. since Vatican II. But, in fairness, there are many places we can look to. Apart from Ireland, most other countries have been through this, and there's any amount of models of how you balance the different roles of the episcopacy and the theologians. The episcopacy have the most important role in Catholic tradition, and they must have a say in theology. Anyone who holds that they won't have a say is looking forward to a future where there will be no theology in the civil educational structures at third level. But the voice of the episcopacy has to be balanced in some manner by the proper pursuit of theology in an academically free environment, in much the same way as other disciplines. But there are models from Germany, England, France, Italy and, indeed, elsewhere which can help us in getting a satisfactory resolution to the question of theology in the civil university in Ireland. And indeed we should look to these now for help.

Geraldine Smyth: On the doubt and faith issue I'm reminded of a saying from one of the primal religious traditions – 'Small doubt, small faith; great doubt, great faith; no doubt, no faith'. So, could we have our next question, please?

Tom Purcell, religion teacher: As one who welcomes the idea of examinations in religious education, I want to address a question to both speakers. Michael Paul Gallagher mentioned a necessity for the healing of cultural blockages – that we need this first as a pre-evangelisation. How are we going to have this when we introduce examinations in religion? Michael Drumm spoke about an enlightened form of theology. Is there going to be a large gap, when we introduce examinations, between ideas like enlightenment and healing on the one hand, and, on the other, the values and practices of an examination culture?

Geraldine Smyth: We'll take a further question to put with that one.

Aidan Donaldson, religion teacher (CBS, Belfast): My question is directed mainly to Michael Paul Gallagher, and it deals with the relationship between culture and society. I was fascinated by his account of the cultural desolation which exists in society. Now, if we do call for a culturally informed and culturally infused faith, are we not coming into conflict with the post-modern society in which we live?

Geraldine Smyth: Maybe Michael Drumm will open the response by addressing the first question about examinations.

Michael Drumm: Well, in an ideal educational world you wouldn't have exams in any subject. But, as many of the experts on assessment will point out to you, non-assessed educational systems ultimately seem to crumble. It would be nice to live in an educational world where Socratic dialogue was the medium for everything, yet the exam seems to insert its greasy paws here as well as elsewhere. I'm afraid this is unavoidable in the kind of world we live in now, with its requirements for accountability etc. And religion in education must ultimately enter into this framework. Obviously, there are all sorts of objections to this type of development on the basis of religious sensibility, and we know them well. Now, it would be interesting to do some research with students of theology at third level at present, say in Mater Dei or Maynooth, to see how they relate their own faith to the examination culture of which they are a part as undergraduates. From my own experience my strong hunch is that, for most students, their faith in God is strengthened rather than weakened by exams!

Michael Paul Gallagher: The question thrown in my direction is a very valid one: How could religion in an examination setting heal the blockages in disposition that I was talking about? In making my response I think I would draw on some catechists, not being a catechist myself. There are two Australian catechists – Graham Rossiter and Monica Crawford – who have written a few very fine books, and whose thoughts I'd like to avail of now. They make a distinction between what they call the potentials of the classroom and the space of a retreat house. The classroom can do certain things. It shouldn't be asked to be a retreat house. A retreat house is a place where you might have a conversion, or learn to pray, or go deeper into your faith. A classroom is a place where you learn to clarify things. But among the things that you clarify are the maps of your own possible spiritual journey, without being pushed into the journey. Out of my relative ignorance, if I had to vote, I would vote for religion being part of an educational system, including examinations, because it would include the knowledge and respectability elements of the subject. Students from the Republic whom I came across in UCD when I taught there didn't know the difference between Ephesians and Ezekiel, but students from Northern Ireland who had ever done any religion in an exam setting at second level did. A knowledge of Scripture is fundamental. If that knowledge comes in a classroom setting, as Rossiter and Crawford would say, then I think we have a good beginning for healing those blockages that lie at the level of disposition.

Quickly, on the second question – doesn't religion come into conflict with post-modernity? I think that on an intellectual level, post-modernity is foe, and on a sensibility level it is friend. I don't take intellectual post-modernity too seriously any more. It was the kind of thing that invaded UCD and the English Department in which I worked, but it died after a few years. But there is an excellent book by a Spanish sociologist, Alejandro Liano, called simply *The New Sensibility: The Positive Side of Postmodernity*. He calls attention to features such as the openness to the spiritual, the feminine as retrieved, the sense of ecology. All these aspects are much more friendly to a deeper and more mature faith. We can be less alarmed about all of postmodernity's accusations of fragmentation on a more intellectual level. So, in brief, it's not all one-way traffic. I think postmodernity can be a friend to a new and quite exciting language of faith.

Geraldine Smith: There's a gentleman in here in the front who is waiting to get in.

Colm McElroy, second-level teacher: I don't teach religion and I'm afraid I don't know the difference between Ephesians and Ezekiel. Fr Michael Paul Gallagher spoke of the dominant kind of unbelief as being cultural. He spoke of cultural desolation and said 'for the younger generation, something is blocking receptivity to the Gospel'. Cultural desolation, he informed us, leaves people untouched with the sense of God which is in everyone. My question is this. Is this view not akin to the fundamentally flawed view of Descartes, '*Cogito ergo sum*', and in the following sense. Fr Michael Paul seems to be making a philosophical claim that something that he construes as religious awareness is present in everyone. Really, I'm asking him if he thinks this is factually true, or is it possible that a human need, or desire, or psychological dependence, could be the cause of man's striving to come to an understanding of God?

Geraldine Smith: We'll take a second question with that one.

Professor Valentine Rice: I work in the 'College of the Holy and Undivided Trinity', which was founded by good Queen Elizabeth many years ago for the advancement of religion and virtue. The two magnificent papers this evening should convince any doubters of the importance of theology in life and in the life of the country. I also find myself in agreement with them about the importance of teaching theology at third level, an importance I would associate with every one of our universities. It's an extraordinary anomaly that the State can pay for what the Americans would call the 'endowment of religion' at primary and post-primary level, but not in third-level institutions. The secular dogma underlying this view is not a peculiarly Irish one. It goes back to the Irish Universities Act of 1908, beyond that to the founding of the Queen's Colleges in the mid-nineteenth century, and beyond that to the founding of the University of London. It held that providing equality of treatment to the different denominations was best achieved by keeping all of them out of the university. I totally endorse the arguments for having the study of theology in our universities funded from public sources and I think a recent court ruling provides the legal basis for doing it.

I would like to go a little bit beyond that however. Towards the end of his talk, Fr Drumm mentioned John Henry Newman. Now Newman wanted something more than the presence of theology in the university. He wanted the interweaving of theology with the other subjects: the cross-fertilisation of theology and the humanities and sciences. In other words, he wanted a Catholic university. And the question I want to raise is: Is the notion of a Catholic university out of date? Is it relevant to us at this particular time in our own country? I was a student in Maynooth many years ago and it was a very wonderful place. In those days there was that intermeshing between the sacred and profane in Maynooth. I cannot be but a bit disappointed with the division that has taken place with more recent developments in Maynooth, with theology identified with the pontifical university and the other subjects identified with the college of the NUI. I wonder if this represents the missing of an opportunity to realise the dream of Newman? Could Maynooth, and should Maynooth, be a Catholic university with the support of the State? I say this of course without any disrespect to other denominations. I really feel however that the recent institutional division introduced in Maynooth may, in the long run, be a bad thing. I'd like to hear our speakers' views.

Geraldine Smyth: Thank you. Could I ask Michael Paul Gallagher to respond to the first question?

Michael Paul Gallagher: I left myself open to that comparison with Descartes. In my rather hurried remarks about the blockage of receptivity, my view of faith must have come across as something narrowly personal, something private that goes on within the lonely individual. The best thing I can offer on Descartes is that he got it wrong largely because his account was in the singular. It should be: '*Cogito, ergo sumus* – I think, therefore *we* are'. We only learn within a community, within a family, or some other grouping. Faith would have its own logic: 'I believe, therefore we love'. That's a Balthasar type logic where he roots the whole act of faith in the first smile of the infant. You put the question: Couldn't all this be psychological dependence? couldn't such dependence explain this particular urge or desire? My response is that it could, if we remain within the level of some vague theism or pagan force that we bow to at various times. The Gospel, however, is very far from psychological dependence. Something happens in the middle of Mark's Gospel – chapter 8 – where they discover who Christ is, and the whole remainder is about letting go of power and control and your very self, and that isn't psychological dependence; that is surrender of the most radical kind. And so in your question you highlight a reductivenesses that we all fall into in our thinking and in our living: of narrowing the horizon to the private, of forgetting the full range of the mystery that invites us, and therefore of speaking a language that is unworthy of the gift that we have been given.

I'll just make one quick comment on the second question, because it's more Michael Drumm's topic. I once wrote an article for an American magazine about the faith in Ireland and I was arguing for the need for theology in the university. I said it was one of the scandals of the NUI that the colleges of this university were forbidden to teach theology. About three months later I got a letter from Africa, from Fr James Good, famous in UCC before he moved to Africa. This friendly but blunt letter said something like this: 'Typical UCD interpretation. UCC had a different interpretation of the NUI Act. I was Professor of Theology there. UCD's view is not the only one.'

Michael Drumm: As a former student of UCC, I can confirm that there was a different interpretation all along in UCC as to what the ban on theology in the 1908 Act meant. In any case the ban wasn't absolute, in that you could have theology taught in the NUI colleges provided that it was funded from 'private benefaction', as the Act put it. So you could have a professor of theology, or any number of them, in an NUI college, provided they weren't funded from the public purse. This is still the case. Another interesting thing in the Act is that any such professor of theology in the NUI couldn't attend faculty meetings. If you could manage such a clause in academic appointments today you'd have no shortage of candidates for the job!

Joking apart, however, the question about the Catholic university is a hugely interesting one from a historical point of view. While I fully appreciate your argument for Maynooth as a Catholic university, I would disagree that this should be the route to take now in our own day. My vision of the future is not that Maynooth should become a Catholic university, but that it should play a full role as a distinctive university in its own right, in the reconstituted NUI which is proposed. This is a role which it could not play as a recognised college of the traditional NUI. The great future there, it seems to me, is that theology can take its rightful place in that system, rather than that theology should colonise study within a Catholic university. Maybe there should have been a Catholic university – and it's interesting to note that St Stephen's Green rather than Maynooth was chosen as the site for Newman's initiative, but the reason that it didn't evolve is a very interesting question in Ireland's educational history. The answer I'd identify as the best one to that question may strike many of you as strange. There is a difference in attitudes between Ireland and other countries which have strong Catholic traditions, such as Belgium, France, Italy, even Holland. In these countries you find a phenomenon amongst Catholics that you never really had in Ireland: that Catholics came together for everything. One of the great strengths of Irish Catholicism, in my view, is that Irish Catholics did not live in an overly clericalised context, despite appearances to the contrary. Irish Catholic education, historically, is not nearly as narrow-minded as many people think. The vast majority of us present came out of it, so unless you're willing to admit that you're essentially narrow-minded yourself, and that your forebears were, then you are going to have to accept that the education system wasn't as narrow-minded as many people later suggested. The reasons why it wasn't are, firstly, that it had many excellent people working in it, but secondly, that public life as a whole didn't get organised along denominational lines as it did in Continental European countries which had strong Catholic traditions. For instance, in Belgium, you had the Catholic pig-farmer's association, you had the Catholic equivalent of the IFA, you had the Catholic trade Unions. They still exist in Italy. One of the triumphs in the Irish historical experience is that sectarianism of this kind was largely avoided in the representative institutions of public life. One area of Irish life where this kind of openness didn't operate to such an extent, as John Coolahan has rightly pointed out, is in education. We don't have Catholic farmers' associations, we don't have Catholic trade unions, and that may be one reason why we won't have a Catholic university.

Geraldine Smyth: Okay, we'll take the next question now.

Tom Corbett: This is an issue which Michael Drumm brought up. It concerns the exploration of cultural influences which are pre-Christian and pagan. And my question is, what value might we expect from going back to examine our ancient Celtic traditions in matters spiritual? Is there anything we might find which would make our dispositions more sensitive to the mystery of Christianity?

Michael Drumm: That's a large question and I'm not exactly sure what the future of such exploration will be. At the very least, however, what cannot be denied is that religion, and religious consciousness understood in a very holistic sense, has made a huge impact on the Irish mind-set over a few millennia. It's to be seen all over the place. There's some very interesting work to be done in this field and I'm trying to do some of it myself in the area of sacramental theology, analysing the rites and rituals of the Irish people. We will at least discover, I think, that Irish Catholicism is a very strange mix of anti-intellectualism on the one hand (which may be one of the reasons why theology has never been fully accepted at third level) and, on the other, something which is extraordinarily practical. For example, I had an exchange student from Switzerland recently and within his first few weeks he said to me: 'This is an awful country. Not only do the people not know when to stand up, sit down, or kneel down at Mass, they know nothing about Scripture'. He came back to me at the end of the year and he apologised. He reflected:

'This is an extraordinary country. The people are quite ignorant in terms of articulating their faith in any theologically acceptable way, but religion here means far more than it does in Switzerland. It's a far more practical and real issue in people's lives. It actually functions as an interpretative model of their lives.' He was telling me, in other words, that it's not something they withdraw to for interesting intellectual discourse. It's something which forms their opinions in a very serious way, particularly at key moments in life. I think Irish Catholicism and its roots is a very rich area. So not only the pre-Christian, but also the Celtic Christian and the later Catholic influences have a lot to tell us that we don't yet appreciate. It is important that theologians carry on this research, and not just anthropologists, historians and archaeologists. This area could open up in a new way if the legal constraints which have hitherto hindered the development of theological research in Ireland could be overcome.

Geraldine Smyth: It remains for me to thank our two speakers. You have already shown in your contributions how much you appreciate what they have had to say this evening. The final question from Tom Corbett, and your response to it, Michael, brought to my own mind the necessity to highlight the importance of imagination in religious consciousness and religious sensibility, and not to leave this altogether to the playwrights and poets. Perhaps there is a sea change afoot in our discourse about God and about meaning. In this connection I think a couple of reflections from Brian Friel are pertinent. He tells us that words are not held fast forever, that they are signals, counters, not immortal. He tells us further that a civilisation can be imprisoned in a linguistic contour which no longer matches the landscape of fact. Both our speakers this evening have taken us into new territory and into a new landscape. They have reminded us that our religious language, nurtured as it is by a Celtic imagination, is full of what Friel calls the 'mythologies of fantasy and hope and self-deception'. And he continues 'a syntax opulent with tomorrows. It is our response to mud cabins and a diet of potatoes; our only method of replying to inevitabilities'. Thank you for your own eloquent replies to what seem to be our own lives' inevitabilities.

4

THE FUTURE OF RELIGION
AT POST-PRIMARY LEVEL

Ann Walsh

'Give me truths, for I am weary of surfaces'
Ralph Waldo Emerson

The majority of the people present at this conference are probably involved in one way or another in the practice of religious education. And already we have had a variety of perspectives from speakers and from the floor. So in making my own presentation I would like to illustrate from the start the perspective from which I speak, and to describe the kinds of things which have influenced me in the approach I take to religious education in the second-level school. There have been four key experiences in recent years which have influenced my attitude to the theme of this conference, and which have also been decisive in shaping my practice as a teacher.

The first of these took place about four years ago when I was showing a video from the *Would You Believe?* series to a fifth-year class. The video dealt with the issue of secular humanism. I was rather proud of refraining from comment myself, in letting the pupils analyse the issues presented in the video and in encouraging them to use their own judgement in deciding about these issues. I had recalled in my own mind some previous critical comments of theirs on a chapter on atheism in their textbook, where they complained: 'This is written completely from a religious point of view'; 'It makes up your mind for you'. So I was keen to let the video run without comment from me. It was a good video, with many frank contributions from people as to why they were agnostic or atheistic. I then gave the pupils an exercise to write on their reactions to the video. Included in the exercise were questions like 'Would you be attracted to the kinds of ideas you have met here?' Their answers communicated boredom and indifference. I was surprised, because I expected that many of them would have been attracted to much of the substance of the video, as pupils five or six years previously would have been. When I questioned them on their reactions, the most typical response was 'Who cares?', 'It doesn't matter', and so on. That, to me, was very revealing and is very much in tune with what Michael Paul Gallagher said last night, namely that outright atheism, in the sense of ideological atheism, is largely a thing of the past. An atheism born of indifference seems to be the much more prevalent mood among young people today. It reminds me of a remark in one of the Vatican II documents – that some never get as far as the point of raising questions about God. They seem to experience no religious stirrings, nor do they sense why they should trouble themselves about religion. It's as if religion is concerned with things that are inane, hardly worth bothering about.

The second experience I want to relate happened seven or eight years ago. I work in a Christian Brothers' school, and the Brothers had commissioned the artist Desmond Kyne to create a stained-glass icon of Edmund Ignatius Rice, the founder of the Order. On the day the finished work was presented to the school the artist himself visited a number of classes and talked about the themes that inspired his work: Celtic themes, the circle of light, and so on. I joined one of these sessions in the morning with a junior class and I was fascinated by the depth and the difficulty of what he was trying to explain. I wondered in the beginning how long he would hold their attention and much to my amazement he thoroughly captivated them. That evening, I had a sixth-year class for the last class – quite a difficult group, and not too bright, if we were to categorise them in rather crude terms. I asked them what they had thought of the artist's session with them and their reaction left an indelible mark on me as a religious educator. They were completely enthralled by what he had said, although his language and concepts were quite difficult, much more difficult than anything I would attempt in class. And when I asked them why the session with the artist had such an effect on them, the nearest one of them came to making a really articulate response was this: 'It would remind you of poetry'. It became obvious to me that the deeper questions of life raised and addressed by the artist were the pupils' questions also. His language and use of symbolism articulated that which found resonance in their own experience. The insight I gained from this, an insight which has governed much of my thinking since, is that so many of our young people lack a language to give voice to experiences which mean something really important to them. The pupil who could find more coherent words than any of his classmates was still struggling to express what the experience with the artist had meant, and the nearest he came to it was to relate it to poetry. While I was amazed at what he had said, I also felt humbled. I had underestimated him, and his fellow pupils. I also felt that in my own teaching I had given the class something which was unworthy of their questions, unworthy of their dignity, and, in fact, of their intelligence. I felt I had trivialised, and indeed tranquillised, the urge towards transcendence which was now clearly in evidence among them, and which I think is latent in everybody.

The third insight comes from one of Cardinal Joseph Ratzinger's texts, *Introduction to Christianity* (1969),[1] where he considers the issue of scandals in the Church. If we look at the high level of hostility and anger levelled at the Church today, and try to gauge the reasons for this, we come across things which are very different from the kind of indifference expressed by young people who are not going to be too stirred by scandals in public institutions, including the Church. In Ratzinger's account, the intensity which characterises anger and hostility towards the

Church generally springs from something other than reasoned arguments. He claims, rather, that it proceeds 'from the bitterness of a broken heart that may have been disappointed in its high hopes, and now, in the pain of a wronged love, can only see the destruction of its love'. I think Ratzinger was right in his analysis here. The kind of anger which is generated by scandal, or by lack of witness, comes from a disappointment which believes that religion ought to have been more, ought to have meant more, ought to have met something better and deeper in us. Now there is a difference between anger of this kind and the cultural desolation which Michael Paul Gallagher spoke about last night. The indifference towards religion among many young people comes closer to this desolation. I do not think that Irish society has come the full way in experiencing this desolation, though I believe it is well on the way, and I expect that teachers of religion will agree with me that they come across increasingly strong evidence of it in their work. Yet, I believe that in Irish society there is still a strong residue of faith – or of a longing that has not been stifled. And there is also the feeling that it has been let down by what religion is seen to offer, much as my sixth years might have been let down by what they perceived I had to offer.

The fourth experience I want to call on is one I had in Seville Lodge. Seville Lodge is an adult education centre in Kilkenny, and every year a seminar is held there for teachers of religion. As a teacher you go there for ideas, especially practical ones to help you motivate your pupils. I remember the most significant experience I had there was a day when Sister Nano Brennan from the Presentation Order of Sisters spoke. In her address she did not give a new blueprint on how to teach pupils on Monday morning – which, to be frank about it, ranks high enough in the expectations of many of us in undertaking such courses. Rather, she gave an account which rejuvenated our sense of what religious education was all about. I realised how bogged down we can become in the routines and mechanics of teaching, and it caused me to rethink my approach in a more fruitful way than would have been possible from the best blueprint or set of new methods that we might have been given. On reflection I have come to believe that religious education is not so much about method as about insight and depth, and secondly, that it's about the kind of thing suggested by Gerard Manley Hopkins' lines: 'There lives the dearest freshness deep down things'.[2] If we have done an injustice in religious education, if the Church has perpetrated any scandal here, I think it is in the trivialisation of religion. That is the injustice I would feel most angry about and would feel the need to apologise for.

Moving on from these four points to some specific issues of religious education at post-primary level, you may have seen a recent article by Joseph Coy in the *Education and Living* supplement of *The Irish Times* (13 February 1996). He claims that there is a crisis in the teaching of the Catholic religion in second-level schools: pupils do not want to study it and teachers do not want to teach it. He mentions problems such as teachers who teach religion in order to fill in gaps on the timetable, competition from other subjects, and the effects of the points race. If we look at the things he has identified and if we consider the comparison between going into a religion class today and two or three decades ago, and take account of the very different atmospheres which prevailed then, we note that it would have been the brave pupil who would have challenged the teacher then; he or she would have been seen as the alienated one. Today, it is almost the reverse. The person who has the courage to stand up and say 'Well, I believe it', is now the one who is different from the rest. And yet I am not so sure that I lament the passing of what seems to have been a more 'religion friendly' era. If we analyse what we might call the props which supported religion and religious education in the past, we find that they were largely concerned with the 'custody of religion', to use a phrase of Pádraig Hogan's.[3] It was largely about maintaining something, controlling something, governing something; a point that was acknowledged last night in the exchange between Michael Drumm and John Coolahan. The very language used, the very experience itself, was very much about having the truth and depositing it, and then feeling a sense of loss when that could not take place any longer. But the props that upheld religious education in the past have largely become redundant. We may well ask if the kinds of symbols and words traditionally used in our schools convey any depth of significance or meaning any more; symbols like crucifixes and other religious emblems, or words like 'salvation', 'redemption'. Are we not left with what Eric Vogelin describes as 'words devoid of meaning', devoid of the original experience that gave rise to them? – left with T.S. Eliot's 'Waste Land'? Indeed we may well ask with him,

> What are the roots that clutch, what branches grow
> Out of this stony rubbish? Son of man,
> You cannot say, or guess, for you know only
> A heap of broken images, where the sun beats,
> And the dead tree gives no shelter, the cricket no relief,
> And the dry stone no sound of water.[4]

It seems to me that this is the kind of situation we are in currently. You'll notice that I'm using poetic images here to try to describe the reality of religious education in our own day. I do so because such images do more justice to the complexity of that reality and allow for a more nuanced understanding of religious education. So if I use a poem of Eliot's to capture the context in which the religious educator works today, I'd also like to draw on another poem to capture the reality of the religious educator herself, or himself. The poem 'Sagart 3' is by Pádraig Daly, an Augustinian who is currently a parish priest in Dublin. He writes of the priest's work, but in terms which are very much akin to the work of the religious educator today:

Like old countrywomen
by fireplaces on Winter evenings
we sit alone.

Outside day draws in: dogs
bark to one another across acres
of mountain. The last red hen
goes wearily to shelter; younger
voices rise and fall in laughter
or argument; there is banging of churns
and milk poured quietly.

We have some urgent tale to tell
about life; but our mouths open
and no sound gathers shape.
We belong out by the side of things.[5]

This line, 'We belong out by the side of things', brings me to the
central point of my contribution this morning, namely that
religious education should be seen as a key element, and not as a
marginal part, of a person's education. And the case I am making
relies on educational and curricular arguments rather than on
any of the traditional props for religion in our schools. The
programme for this conference lists some of these props: for
instance, the prevalence of religious in principalships, the almost
exclusive clerical control of management, the regular conduct of
religious observances within schools, and so on. I do not regret
or fear the passing of such supports. They may have been
appropriate for another time. I would much prefer, however, to
place the emphasis in religious education on the quality of the
religious influences actually experienced by pupils in schools, and
also on the rationale for religion in the curriculum. Accordingly,
I welcome the opening up of the religious question within the
educational arena.

This opening up is a relatively new development. Those who were involved in previous efforts to draw up a religious education programme for the Leaving Certificate were struck by the paucity of knowledge in the Department of Education about religion as an area of study. This paucity was contributed to by two main factors in my view – firstly, a general non-interest in the question by officials and successive ministers; but secondly, as last night's discussions emphasised, the strong message given by religious authorities that religious education was their preserve, was in their custody. For these reasons I would indeed welcome the passing away of the traditional props and the breaking forth of religion in a new way into the mainstream of Irish society, into the mainstream of educational discourse and, in particular, into the mainstream of deliberations about the curriculum. I do not think we have anything to fear from that, rather the reverse.

In this connection it is still true, of course, that there is little explicit reference to religion in the Green Paper of 1992, *Education for a Changing World,* or the White Paper of 1995, *Charting our Education Future.* But despite these omissions, the reasons for which I referred to a little earlier, there are other recent developments which are really promising. Consider for instance the main aim of education adopted by the National Council for Curriculum and Assessment, cited in virtually all of their documents, and which is now beginning to be cited by the Department of Education:

> The general aim of education is to contribute to the development of all aspects of the individual, including aesthetic, creative, critical, cultural, emotional, intellectual, moral, physical, political, social and spiritual development, for personal and family life, for working life, for living in the community, and for leisure.

I welcome this definition of education. If we recall the debate on the Green Paper, we note that its assertive utilitarian note, the so-called 'enterprise culture' announced first by the then Minister, Seamus Brennan, called forth a disapproving response from a very wide range of interests in Irish education. The National Education Convention offered opportunities for these responses to be articulated further and shared with others. It was impressed upon officials and policymakers during these deliberations that the main representative bodies of the Irish public, and not just of Irish education, were not happy with the functionalist view of education canvassed by the Green Paper. And the fruits of these deliberations are evident in the fact that the 1995 White Paper has largely moved away from the utilitarian thrust and embraces a more philosophical and holistic approach. In this I think we have a lot to be happy about, and, indeed, much to build on in the future.

This kind of new and open framework, which will probably be enshrined in law before long, allows religion its own role and its own voice, or, to use a phrase by theologian James Mackey, allows 'equality of citizenship for faith as a way of interpreting experience'. The definition itself suggests that education as an enterprise would be somewhat lacking if it did not address the moral and spiritual dimensions of the person. This new sense of equality for religious education is very different from the older sense of exclusiveness, of having the final truth to transmit, which provoked so many of the reactions which are hostile to the presence of religious education in the schools.

But promising as these developments are in offering and preserving a new definition of religious education, I think we still need to move beyond them. The lack of theological literacy in Irish society was mentioned more than once in last night's discussions, and I am concerned by this lack of literacy. It pervades all aspects of life, including current affairs programmes on the radio and television, where one expects the contributions of participants, and at least those of the programme presenters, to be reasonably well-informed. Let me give you an example. On a recent edition of a popular current affairs radio programme I heard the presenter (who prides himself on researching his subject well if it happens to be politics, economics, literature, music or whatever) ask his interviewee if, when a Church holiday falls on a Saturday, attendance at the vigil Mass on Saturday satisfies the obligation for both days; could you get 'two for the price of one'? Now, it may seem an insignificant example, but in what other walk of life would such flippancy, such paucity of knowledge, be admired, welcomed or tolerated? I do not think that society has anything to gain by being theologically illiterate. Equally, I do not think Church authorities have anything to fear from lay people becoming theologically literate.

That is why, in talking about the future of religious education in our schools, I fail to get exercised by debates about whether or not religion should be an examination subject. Similarly, I find it difficult to go along with the alleged differences and polarisations between religious education, religious studies, catechesis. Why? Because I think the whole enterprise goes much deeper than these distinctions and these debates. The enterprise of religious education is inseparable from the philosophical question: What is the meaning of life? And this question exists whoever you are, or whatever you are. The search for truth, for meaning, goes right back to Greek-Socratic culture and beyond. And whatever audience may be in front of me this morning, or in front of any of us as teachers, I do not think anyone is immune to that question.

The American writer James Fowler talks, at the beginning of the book *Stages of Faith,*[6] of preparing to conduct a seminar. He devises a set of questions for participants: 'What commands your best attention?' 'What dreams and hopes do you have?' 'What are you pouring your life out for?' Then he pulls himself up short and asks himself: 'How would I answer these questions?' And those are questions that remain relevant for everyone, no matter who you are in terms of intellect, or interest, or abilities or whatever. How should my life be lived? I think that's the core at which we should begin religious education. And it is sad that the kind of religious education we have had may have trivialised that question, as I suggested earlier in my remarks; that it may have caught up the essence of that question into what has now become a series of empty images.

To put all of this in very familiar terms, it is the kind of question that Shirley Valentine reflects on in the film *Shirley Valentine* as she finds herself sipping wine overlooking the Mediterranean, realising that she has become fed up with her mundane life. 'I've led such a little life', she says, 'and even that'll be over pretty soon. I've allowed myself to lead this little life when inside me there's so much more and it's all gone unused and now it will never be used. Why do we get all this life if we don't ever use it? Why do we get all these feelings and dreams and hopes if we don't ever use them? That's where Shirley Valentine disappeared to – she got lost in all this unused life'. Again, this shows us the primary location for religious education. The loss she refers to was alluded to in different ways in the references to cultural desolation last night, and in my own references a little earlier to the indifference I encountered in the pupils to whom I showed the video. Addressing this loss is the real issue concerning religious education and it seems a really daunting task. On the other hand however, it has to be possible, because time and time again the central question – what is the meaning of life? – raises its head despite all the forces that seek to deaden it. The task of religious education is one of clearing the debris, removing the obstacles and allowing the innate urge towards the transcendent to emerge.

A book I have been reading recently, *Mortally Wounded* by Dr Michael Kearney, who is Director of the Hospice in Harold's Cross, gives a further illuminating perspective on the question I am trying to formulate.[7] The book deals essentially with its author's experiences with the dying. He examines the reality of death, not necessarily from a religious point of view, but not excluding it either, and he puts before our consideration the thesis that to die well is somehow linked to having come to an awareness of depths within oneself. Now that is religious in the broadest sense, though in treating his theme, Kearney offers insights from Greek myths, from the Buddhist tradition, from primal religious traditions and so on. In particular, he talks about the whole area of the search for truth and meaning which attends life with a particular urgency when death is close at hand and approaching ever nearer. What is my life about? What is its value, its significance, its merit? How can I be happy?

In Irish society, philosophical questions of this kind have rarely enough been given explicit articulation, and religious education, properly understood and conducted, can provide real and practical ways of meeting these questions. In other countries, France for example, philosophical questions are no strangers to the culture generally, and the tools for questioning are no stranger to the educational system. In Ireland, by contrast, the tradition has been more one of supplying ready-made answers than pursuing questions, and our educational system has not, by and large, been quick to encourage the language, or the grammar, of questioning. But that is the road we now have to follow, in my view. And one of the practical consequences of taking this route is that religion becomes a subject in the certificate examinations. But the exam should not the big issue here. Properly viewed, the serious study of religion at this level should provide the means by which an informed faith is possible. It may remove some of the obstacles that hinder the possibility of faith. And how? By bringing people back to face some of the fundamental questions, even at the level of argument. How many of us, and of our pupils, operate from cliché, from superficial thinking? In this kind of context if you push people to consider the consequences of their viewpoint, they are lost. It is our failure to push, to make connections between our pupils' experiences and those of people some thousands of miles away or some thousands of years ago, that needs to be put right. The questions of life and the purpose of life are as old as time itself, and the purpose of religious education is to bring people into touch with these deeper questions in a serious and sustained way.

I have been involved in the last few years in preparing textbooks for religion which seek to challenge pupils intellectually as well as spiritually. In my teaching I have used these texts with those who would be regarded as very weak pupils. This is not to do anything so crude, I hope, as to praise the merits of my own texts, but rather to say that where depth is concerned, if the conviction lies within yourself, if the search is there, you'll find a way of making real contact with the pupils. The best moments in my life as a teacher have been those when I spoke from a sense of depth and when I knew from the reactions in my pupils' eyes that they knew what I was talking about. I'm not saying they could articulate or explain it, but they knew, deep down, what I was talking about.

So, in conclusion, let me recall in a fuller context now the title of this address, which is a little abbreviated, because Emerson's full quotation was: 'Give me truths, for I am weary of surfaces, and die of inanition'. This suggests rather powerfully to me where religious education should be heading in the future. From what I have said already it should be clear that I do not have in mind here religion as a deposit of truths to hand down in a crude and definite way, but rather the kind of journey the Italian poet Margherita Guidacci brings before us when she writes:

> persevere, traveller,
> to the very end, though you have
> no other guide but your anxiety
> and dismay. Truth awaits man, but awaits him only
> when his last step has been taken.[8]

5

WHITHER THE FOURTH R? A PERSPECTIVE ON THE FUTURE OF RELIGION IN PRIMARY SCHOOLS

Kieran Griffin

Introduction

This paper seeks, firstly, to draw on the contrasting positions of the teaching of religion within the educational systems of the Republic of Ireland and the United States of America in the light of recent developments in both countries. Secondly, it attempts to indicate a possible future direction for the Irish system which, if acceptable and implemented, would lead to more inclusive schools.

The constitutional parameters within which the position of religion in schools in both countries is bound appear remarkably similar. Article 44.2.1. of the Irish Constitution states that 'the free profession and practice of religion are ... guaranteed to every citizen' and Article 44.2.2. states that 'the State guarantees not to endow any religion'.[1] In the United States, the First Amendment to the Constitution declares that 'Congress shall make no law respecting an establishment of religion, or prohibiting the free exercise thereof'.[2] Despite these similarities, the manner in which the constitutions have been interpreted in both jurisdictions has resulted in the issue of religion in schools being treated in exactly the opposite manner in the two countries. In Ireland religion is considered 'by far the most important' part of the school curriculum,[3] whereas in the US its teaching is prohibited in all public schools.

Before expanding on the contrasting treatment of religion in schools in Ireland and the US, a further dimension of the issue needs to be considered, namely, calls within both countries for a change in the status quo. In the Republic of Ireland calls for change from such groups as the Campaign to Separate Church and State and the multi-denominational movement have become increasingly noticeable in the public and educational domains.[4] In the US groups such as the Anti-Defamation League document the frequent challenges by minority groups, at State and Federal Court level, to the exclusion of religion from schools.[5]

Apart from the constitutional contexts and the campaigns for change, other factors need to inform an understanding of religion in schools. Particular to the Irish context have been the recent decades of violence, mostly confined to Northern Ireland, followed by eighteen months of relative peace, which was in turn shattered by the IRA bombing of Canary Wharf in February 1996. Throughout much of the period of violence efforts were made, and continue to be made, to bridge sectarian divisions through educational initiatives such as the Integrated Education movement in Northern Ireland. This encourages the establishment of inter-denominational schools and the cross-curricular initiative called 'Education for Mutual Understanding', which is now part of the National Curriculum in Northern Ireland. Related to these developments has been the founding of fourteen multi-denominational primary schools in the Republic of Ireland in the period 1978 to the present day. Having set the background to my address with these introductory remarks, let me now look at some specific issues which are central to my theme.

The issue of chaplains in schools

The Campaign to Separate Church and State and Mr Jeremiah Noel Murphy recently sought in the Irish High Court a declaration that the payment by the Department of Education of the salaries of chaplains employed in post-primary schools known as community schools breached the provisions of Article 44.2.2. of the Constitution, by which the State guarantees 'not to endow any religion'. Mr Justice Costello refused the plaintiffs' case. In the course of his judgment he stated:

> [I]t is clear that one of the important reasons why chaplains as well as teachers are appointed to the staff of community schools is for the purpose of assisting the religious formation of the children attending the school (assistance which, *inter alia,* is given by the celebration of Mass in the school). In effect, the State, by paying the salaries for chaplains, is having regard to the rights of parents *vis-à-vis* the religious formation of their children and enabling them to exercise their constitutionally recognised rights. If this is the purpose and effect of the the payment how can it be said it is unconstitutional.[6]

The judgment also contained references to the US Constitution and the judge noted that the concepts 'endowment' and 'establishment', when applied to religion, were, 'as a matter of Irish law, distinct and different'.[7] The judgment allows the Irish State not only to pay chaplains, or other religious or lay persons, to familiarise children with religious doctrine, apologetics, historical and comparative religion, but also to pay such persons to inculcate religious practice such as prayer or Mass.

The original defendant in this case was the Minister for Education. At its own request the Roman Catholic Church was enjoined as a defendant, as a 'substantial financial loss would be suffered' if the claim were to be allowed.[8] Church involvement and interest in Irish education, since its formal inception in 1831, runs far deeper than would be indicated by financial gain or loss, and the willingness to to defend this case would indicate a desire to maintain Church's involvement at its historical level.

In addition to the four metropolitan archbishops of the Roman Catholic Church, the Church of Ireland also instructed counsel for the defence.

The plaintiffs had to accept that the Court's judgment that State financial aid to religious or denominational schools and the payment of salaries of teachers of religion did not amount to an 'endowment of religion' and therefore were not prohibited by the Constitution. Barring a successful appeal of this judgment in the Supreme Court, the position of religious communities in Irish schools and the teaching of denominational religion to children in State-aided schools would seem set to continue as heretofore, with the added protection of an emphatic court determination of the constitutionality of this position.

The Lemon Test

In 1971 the US Supreme Court declared unconstitutional the Pennsylvania statute which authorised the State to reimburse non-public schools in which religion was taught for the cost of secular educational services. The particular case was *Lemon v. Kurtzman.*[9] The judgement in the case, which became known as the 'Lemon Test', provides that 'to pass constitutional muster a government practice challenged under the establishment clause must have a secular purpose; it must have the primary effect which neither advances nor inhibits religion: and it must avoid excessive entanglement with religion'.[10]

A variety of issues regarding the constutionality of practices relating to religion in schools has exercised the courts in the US and continues to do so. The following examples are a small selection:

> *Wallace* v. *Felton* (1985) – Alabama 'moment of silence' statute was ruled unconstitutional;

> *Lee* v. *Wiseman* (1992) – Prayer at public school graduation ceremonies was ruled unconstitutional;

Kiryas Joel v. *Grumet* – A village school district which was created to conform to the boundaries of a Hasidic community was ruled unconstitutional.[11]

Individual rights to the expression of religion have been upheld in US courts. Private, individual and voluntary prayer are allowed. It is permissible to teach about religion. The Bible may be treated for study purposes as literature. Students may be released for religious classes which take place off the school premises. Under an Equal Access Act (1984) religious clubs initiated by students must be treated in the same manner as other student clubs – political, sporting and such.

These examples show that US public schools offer a complete contrast to Irish schools in the matter of the treatment of religion. The different meanings in law of the terms 'establishment' and 'endowment', and their different interpretations in Irish and US courts, have given rise to this contrast. These differences were clearly understood and debated, according to Justice Costello in his judgment in the school chaplains case.[12] (Clear antecedents existed in the 1922 and 1937 Irish Constitutions, in the Home Rule Bill of 1893, in the Government of Ireland Act, 1914 and in the Government of Ireland Act, 1920, all of which used a clause prohibiting the making of a law 'respecting the establishment or endowment of religion').[13]

Chains or change?

The present educational system in Ireland is the product of approximately two centuries of designed and accidental development. It bears many of the hallmarks of historical decisions, omissions and traditions. If it were to be radically altered it is unlikely that its present state would provide a useful starting-point. The attempt by the plaintiffs in the school chaplains case in the High Court was clearly an effort to change the system into a US type system and that effort failed. Yet all systems of education are subject to change. Changes in family, society, politics and demographics bring tensions to bear on systems and inevitably bring about change in the systems themselves.

Of profound importance to education in Ireland in this respect has been the emergence of the voice of parents in education. The situation which obtained prior to this recent emergence was highlighted in an article by Gerry Whyte in *The Irish Jurist* in 1992. He wrote:

> [T]he constitutional model of education placed parents at the apex of the system, with the State in a supportive role … the reality was quite different, with parents essentially the silent partners in a system dominated by the school managers and the Department of Education. The explanation of this discrepancy would appear to lie in the significance of the historical context for the interpretation of these constitutional provisions. The context was one in which the interests of parents and of the Churches could be regarded as synonymous, with the result that references to parents' rights in Article 42 could be regarded as constitutional protection, by proxy as it were, for the interests of the Churches.[14]

Such a context clearly no longer obtains. Parents now speak for themselves through the National Parents' Council, through parents' asociations, through their limited role on school boards, through their actions in setting up Gaelscoileanna and multi-denominational schools. This emergence of a stronger voice for parents has created tensions between parents' representatives and the Churches on the question of the governance of schools. The Report on the National Education Convention (1994) notes:

The teachers and most parents seek equal repersentation with trustees' or patrons' nominees on the Boards. The majority of trustees/patrons are reluctant to depart from a guarantee of a majority of nominees on the Boards and the appointment of a Chairperson, in the interests of protecting their denominational concerns.[15]

The Churches' stated *raison d'être* for the role they play in controlling schools is that they comply with parental wishes in the religious education of children. Yet when parents wish to have equal say in the control of schools the Churches have refused them. Sometimes the defence of this position can seem obscure, if not condescending. For instance, Sr Eileen Randles, General Secretary of the Catholic Primary School Managers' Association (CPSMA) wrote in an article in *The Irish Times* in November 1993:

> Do the local people, as distinct from the media, really want the bishop to stop co-ordinating the efforts needed to provide and maintain a Catholic school in the parish? Who will do it instead? We're told that parents who try to establish a school of their own find it difficult to deal with the legal and financial issues involved, and this is not surprising given the increasing complexity of the issues.[16]

According to a post-budget supplement in *The Irish Times* in January 1996, the CPSMA itself called for the abolition of the local contribution paid by parishes and its replacement by State funds.[17]

Within the Churches, changing circumstances and perceptions have caused some commentators to consider anew the traditional position of their organisation' roles in education. At the Patrick McGill Summer School in 1989, Bishop Brendan Comiskey, the Catholic Bishop of Ferns, had the following to say:

A Church, or a religious institution, or indeed an individual, who continues to do unthinkingly what he, she, or it always did, is writing its own obituary. Certainly the numbers game is causing many religious educators to have second thoughts. But many good and loving educators are having second thoughts when they look into the eyes of their younger brothers and sisters and see the lines on those faces written by changes in today's world. What they see in those faces, and how they respond, more than any desire to 'control education', will determine the involvement of religious in education as we move towards the end of this century.[18]

Thus the views of significant spokespersons for the largest Church grouping in Ireland, the Roman Catholic Church, would appear to differ. On the one hand, we have one spokesperson indicating that only bishops were capable of organising schools and on the other, we have a bishop indicating the need for a rethink of the Church's position.

The multi-denominational movement

There are fourteen multi-denominational primary schools in the Republic of Ireland. They were founded by parents, are managed by parents, and are recognised for the purpose of funding and regulating by the State in the same manner as other primary schools in the National School system.

The emergence and history of the first of these schools, the Dalkey School Project, founded in 1978, has been documented.[19] A number of aspects of this prototype are noteworthy in the context of this paper. Firstly, the movement for multi-denominational education (defined as giving equal access and treatment within school to children of any or no religion), and the founding of the first such primary school, emerged out of a denominational school. The majority of parents of pupils in St Patrick's National School in Dalkey, Co. Dublin, which was under the patronage and management of the Church of Ireland, disputed the Church's authority to exclude from the school children of other religions or of none. Secondly, the movement was driven by parents. Thirdly, those involved – parents and teachers – developed an agreed religious education programme known as the core curriculum in religious education. This seeks to educate children about religion and about its place in their community and in society at large, but it is not a confessional programme. Nor does it seek to instruct the children in the tenets of any one belief system. Finally, a facility is granted to parents to organise faith groups for the purpose of providing particular instruction/formation within the school premises either outside school hours, or within school hours where timetabling and space considerations allow.

The other multi-denominational schools grew out of the success of the Dalkey School Project National School and its first successors. Although they did not emerge from a previously existing denominational school, they would share with the Dalkey School Project the other features alluded to above.

Two indicators of the success and acceptance of these schools are the demand for places in them – which outstrips the ability of the schools to provide such spaces – and the reported majority of teachers in a recent national survey who wanted multi-denominational schools. In the school where I am Principal, the Bray School Project, demand for places in the reception class outstrips the number of places available by by about four to one. In a recent unpublished survey of parents in the same school, 66 per cent of respondents indicated that their main reason for sending their children to the school was because it was multi-denominational, compared to 10 per cent whose primary reason was the school's reputation, and a further 10 per cent whose primary reason was because of its democratic structure – i.e the involvement of parents. In a recent survey conducted by the

INTO among its members, a majority of teachers are reported to prefer to work in a multi-denominational school than in a denominational school.[20]

Conclusions – towards inclusive schools

While the aim of the legal challenge to the position of religion in Irish schools would appear to be that of replacing the current position with a US type position, it is unlikely that such a radical change would enjoy widespread support. If, however, the parents of all children in primary or second-level schools were asked whether their preference was for the retention of the denominational model or a change to a multi-denominational model, it is probable that a significant number would opt for the change. In a small number of schools it is probable that a majority of parents would opt for such a change. In the vast majority of schools, it is probable that at least some parents would opt for such a change. It is inconceivable that the State would be asked to provide separately for such people where they do not have access to a multi-denominational school, since this would require the replication of a majority of schools.

The implementation to the limit of what is legally permissible with regard to religion in Irish schools excludes some children from full participation in the schools they attend. In a time of debate about the governance of schools and the relevant roles of the various partners – the Churches, parents, teachers and, where appropriate, the children – it is opportune to consider whether all children can be equally accommodated in schools. In California, a response to the debate about religion in schools has been the 'California 3 Rs project'.[21] This proposes that the guiding principles for living with differences should be based on rights, responsibilities and respect – the right to religious liberty or freedom of conscience, the responsibility to respect that right in others and the necessity of respecting the convictions of others.

The adoption of a charter for practice in Irish schools based on such principles might logically lead to an examination of the confessional nature of the treatment of religion in most schools. An option similar to the core curriculum in religious education might be developed by the various partners in schools. This would seek to acquaint children with beliefs they share and those they don't, and would thus treat religion in schools as a secular subject. A fourth 'R', the right to instruction for those who seek it, might also accommodate a solution to a problem, if one exists, for those who would prefer no change in the system. Such measures would not seek to minimise, ignore or trivialise differences, but would recognise them, as well as affirm what is shared. Schools committed to the development of an inclusive ethos would treat all of the children equally and would not exclude some children, at least from part of the curriculum, by virtue of their not being of the majority religion of their school.

At a time when curricula and structures, including governing structures, are being examined with a view to the educational system gearing itself for the twenty-first century, the measures just recommended would involve a difference in only one subject – religious education – and a change of attitude in our schools towards minorities, thus making them inclusive schools.

6

SUBJECTS OR ARCHITECTS OF CULTURE? RELIGIOUS EDUCATION AND CHILDREN'S EXPERIENCE

Tom Larkin

Introduction

There is a question behind the title of the conference – Does religion have a future in Irish Education? My answer is 'Yes, but…' I will approach this question drawing on my experience as a teacher in the primary sector. I intend to look in some detail at 'culture' because, as American sociologist George Gerbner said, 'What people learn best is not what teachers think they teach, or what their preachers think they preach, but what their cultures in fact cultivate.'[1]

Beginning with some perspectives on culture, in order to clarify our understanding of what it is, I will then go on to look at the concept of 'world view' and the phenomenon of religion in that context. Then, taking the title 'The state we're in', I will briefly outline some contemporary problems at global and national levels before examining more particularly the culture of the middle primary classroom. The core of my argument will be that if religion has a future in Irish education, then it must first address itself to the problems we share as a people. Secondly, it must begin in the communities where the children live – primarily with parents – in order to provide a context for the work which can appropriately be done in the school.

Culture – 'The way we do things 'round here'

Let's start with a story. The story goes like this. A long time ago, there lived a group of people in a mountainous region, where there were also many lions. Often at night the lions would attack the weak and elderly who lived in huts at the edge of the village. The community met to discuss how they would cope with this problem. They decided to build a fence around the entire village, with only one gate in the fence. However, no one in particular had been given the responsibility for closing the gate. It was often left open and people were still being killed. So they met again and decided that the second son of each family would take it in turns to close the gate. They did this and no more people were killed. Now these people were hunters and about a hundred years after making this decision they had killed all the lions in the area. Two hundred years later, no one in the village could remember that there had been lions in the mountains. Even so, the second sons are still closing the gate every night. When they ask why, the elders reply 'That's the way we do things 'round here.' 'The way we do things 'round here' is the best indicator of a group's or society's culture. Culture is one of the most difficult words to define. Most definitions include some or all of the following elements: world view and lifestyle; beliefs, values, customs, traditions and artefacts; way of life; patterns of thought and behaviour; meanings attached to different phenomena; organisation of relationships and roles at social, economic, political, ecological and religious levels; patterns of meaning embodied in symbols; solutions to problems related to basic needs etc. All of these are learned and held in common by a society or group.

A useful image for looking at culture is that of an iceberg (Fig. 1). Culture is like an iceberg in that only 10 per cent of it is visible – music, food, art, clothes etc. About 90 per cent of what constitutes culture is beyond or below our conscious awareness – how we value ourselves and others, how problems are solved, customs around birth, death and marriage, etc. These more subtle, or less visible aspects are powerful and pervasive and, although they are less obvious, they tend to have the strongest effect on our lives.

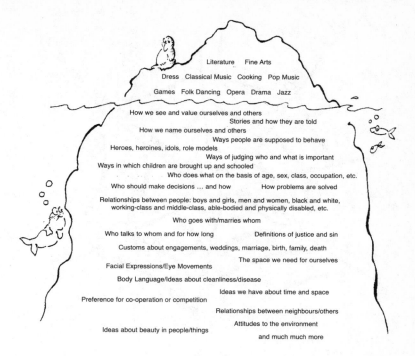

Fig. 1[2]

Another image is the spider's web (Fig. 2). This model allows us to recognise that culture is flexible, yet integrated. The key, or anchor strands, in the web reflect the main structures or systems around which society is organised. Each one affects the other. A shift in any one strand creates ripples in all the others, e.g. changes in the way we see the environment have led to changes in our patterns of consumption and to changes in the political system.

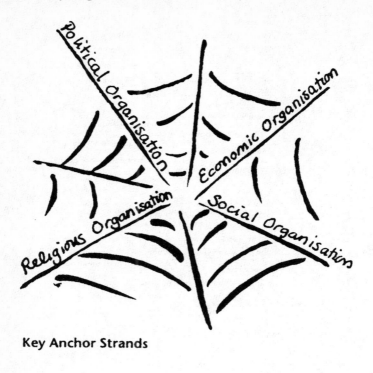

Key Anchor Strands

Fig. 2[3]

We are not born 'with' culture – we must learn our culture through a process of enculturation. This happens through a combination of conscious and unconscious means, formal and informal. It is taught to us overtly as children in our families. We are 'coached' in culture. However, this is just a small part of what we learn. As a result of listening and watching, children imitate, often unconsciously, the behaviour of other children and adults around them – including those on television. Children encode the signals for a variety of expressions and behaviours, e.g. yawning when bored, without anyone actually teaching them. Like sponges, they simply absorb them as well as a great deal more of cultural learning. Paul Andrews has recently made some incisive observations in this connection.

> Obviously, parents influence their children more by what they are than by what they say. The theories we use for rearing children are constantly falling foul of the unconscious assumptions on which we act all day long. So parents who are determined to bring up their family in a different style from that in which they were reared, may find later, to their discomfort, that they are addressing their children in the tone and sometimes even the words of their own parents.[4]

The important thing here is that we learn our culture, that it is not something innate or static, not a finished product, but is always in process, is always affecting us and shaping us. However, this is not a one-way process; we can and do actively produce and shape our culture too. We can be 'architects of culture'.

World view and religion

One very important cultural construct we learn is a world view. This is the ongoing product of a process whereby we imagine the world. It is the story we tell ourselves about the world and our place in it. It acts as a framework for organising our experience. It includes our values, attitudes and assumptions about the nature of reality, about the significance of human life, about power and change and about right and wrong. Each society, and each individual in a society, has a world view which helps to make sense of reality and engenders confidence in our ability to deal with that reality. A useful way of looking at the importance of world view in relation to culture is Donal Jacob's scheme of the levels of culture, representing progressive interiority.

Level 1 – Industrial–Technical: This level includes the organisation and techniques of the economic world: industry; business and commerce; work, or the lack of work; the mass media; travel; sport etc.

Level 2 – Domestic-Technical: This level contains customs, traditions, lifestyles, use of leisure time etc. It is associated with home and family life

Level 3 – Values: This is the cohesive or 'glue' element of a culture. Through values, we decide priorities and make characteristic choices when confronted with alternatives.

Level 4 – World view: Every culture seeks to present a common, integrated world view. This is at the very heart of culture and it is at this deep level that we place religious experience and understanding.[5]

Among other things, religion provides believers with the terms and meaning of existence; it helps believers to intensify and unify their experience of faith and action; it offers believers a rule and framework for life at personal and social levels; it is concerned with some ultimate power beyond the human and natural worlds; it performs an integrating function through its symbols, rituals, beliefs and organisation. In the recent past, at least in Ireland, if not across the greater part of Europe, the world view of society was largely a religious one.

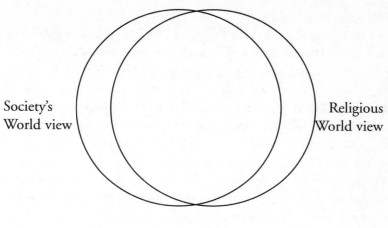

Fig. 3[6]

Of course, religion is perceived in this traditional picture as being very concerned with structure; buildings, rituals, numbers etc. where the job of lay people was to 'pray, pay and obey'. Today, with the plurality of sub-cultures and the weakening of religious influence the picture probably looks more like this:

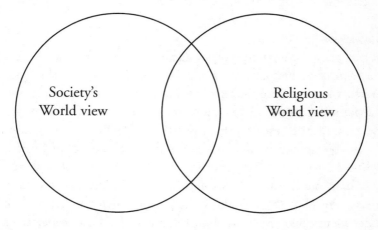

Fig. 4[7]

The state we're in

In examining the role and future of religion in education, it is necessary to look briefly at the socio-economic/political situation. But first, a story: One night, a garda was on the beat. Under a street lamp he came across a man on his hands and knees, apparently looking for something. The garda enquired, 'What are you doing there?' 'I'm looking for my keys', the man replied. So the garda got down on his hands and knees and proceeded to look for the man's keys. Having painstakingly combed the area around the street lamp, the garda asked, 'Are you sure you lost them around here?' To which the man responded, 'Oh no, I lost them way back there.' 'Then why are you looking for them here?' asked the garda. 'Well', the man replied, 'it was too dark back there, and there's plenty of light here.'

Unlike the man who searches only where the light shines, if we are to find the keys and solutions to the problems that beset us (which is one of the basic functions of any culture), then we must uncover where these keys actually are, even if they have largely been overlooked by our culture. As I suggested at the beginning, this effort to uncover and understand has three dimensions – global, national and local.

Global dimension

At first glance, the picture of the earth is quite bleak: there is still the increasing disparity between the rich North and the poor South; there is a proliferation of wars, fuelled by a flourishing international arms trade; the horror of famine, or, rather, starvation; the escalating numbers of refugees; ongoing, irreversible ecological destruction; widespread abuses of human rights and so on. It is almost too easy to lengthen this catalogue of human-made disasters. Western civilisation appears to be at a crisis point. This crisis is not merely economic or political. The issues mentioned above are symptomatic of an even deeper crisis which is cultural.

National dimension

While not as apocalyptic, the picture of Ireland is not all that much brighter. The island is beset by many problems which are constantly increasing: poverty, unemployment, crime, drugs, domestic violence, violence related to Northern Ireland, suicide, environmental degradation, racism etc. These both reflect and create an increasingly polarised society. And all this before we make reference to consumerism, materialism and secularism. In the face of these problems, is it any wonder that many of our young people experience powerlessness, disillusionment, alienation, hopelessness and apathy? Again, it is to the deeper level of culture that we must turn in an attempt to understand this crisis – to the realm of meaning and values and their absence.

We can take some comfort from the fact that numerous responses have been and are being made to these problems at global, national and local levels. All of these responses are characterised by basic concern, solidarity and enlightened self-interest; from the United Nations, Earth Summit and Beijing Women's Conference through campaign groups like Greenpeace and Amnesty International to local church and community groups, all display 'the passion to make and make again, where such unmaking reigns.'[8] It is when people work with each other to solve common problems that they can regain a sense of meaning and direction in a world out of kilter.

Classroom dimension

At the local level, the public at large turns its collective eye on the education system, sometimes to point the finger of blame, but more often to seek a solution to the ills of society. However, the classroom itself is not exempt from the issues and concerns of the world; in microcosm it reflects many of the problems which occupy the broader stage, particularly at the level of the culture of the classroom. It is on this aspect that I would like to place a special focus.

Realities and possibilities of the classroom

I'd like to believe that the classes I have taught have been characterised by co-operation, enthusiasm, compassion, listening, generosity and wonder. However, while these qualities were present in some measure, the culture of the classroom, as exhibited by a significant minority of the children, is more frequently characterised by the less desirable values of:

- competitiveness – most children want to be first or best in anything and everything, often aggressively so;
- ruthlessness – mistakes are opportunities for 'slagging' and put-downs. Differences are pounced on and emphasised or punished;
- constant babble – everyone tries to talk and be heard at the same time – the 'Den TV' syndrome;
- lack of concentration – this refers both to short attention span and to 'faddism', where they move from one thing to another at the whim of advertisers, e.g. from 'POGS' to 'Premier League Stickers';
- lack of loyalty – anyone who does anything wrong gets 'ratted on', not just by one person, but by many;
- 'mé féin-ism' – the philosophy here seems to be 'get as much as you can of whatever is going, and don't share any of it.' This acquisitiveness also extends to the attention of whatever adults happen to be around.

From my experience of meeting with and listening to other teachers, I am reliably informed that this picture is not exclusive to suburban Dublin. I devised and taught a programme of structured learning experiences – in the context of religious education – to address some of the values and behaviours listed above. Things did change in the classroom, while I was there, but in the yard and after school the situation reverted – 'It's the way they do things 'round here'.

Looking back over the years, one thing that struck me about

the situations which I have described is that there was/is something very 'male' about them. Recently I asked the children about the videos they watch. Girls mentioned Disney movies – like *The Little Mermaid* and *Beauty and the Beast,* along with others such as *Little Women* and *The Secret Garden.* Boys, on the other hand, listed *Terminator, Demolition Man* and *Jurassic Park.* Girls preferred films like *Pocahontas* and *The Little Princess,* whereas boys wanted to see *Batman Forever* or *Die Hard With a Vengeance.* When I asked the children to write stories, boys wrote only about males, while girls usually wrote about both sexes. Something similar happened when I asked them to draw pictures.

Girls and boys in school are, for the most part, products of a shared culture. However, each appears to belong to a particular sub-culture. Thorne's researches of behaviour patterns in girls and boys in the United States draws the following contrasts:[9]

Girls mix in smaller groups or pairs; they focus on relationships; they play co-operatively and take turns; they are concerned about harmony; they chat about their family and friends; they are process-oriented; they use a language of inclusion and suggestion.	Boys mix in larger groups or gangs; they focus on things and machines; they play rough and tumble; they are concerned about winning; they get involved easily in conflict; they are action-oriented, or task-oriented; they use a language of command, challenge or insult.

While not all girls' and boys' behaviour conforms to these stereotypic descriptions, unfortunately, in my experience, most do. Interestingly, girls are much more open to change and to extending their repertoire of activities, whereas boys seem to get 'stuck' or 'fixed'.

Kathleen McDonnell, in her surveys of children's culture, suggests that 'the 'problem' lies less with the fact that boys and girls prefer different realms, than with the low esteem in which girls' culture is almost universally held.'[10] Boys' culture is seen as a problem, because it seems to glorify violence. A walk through any toyshop shows this clearly. Boys' toys tend to be black or dark in colour, aggressive in stance and grim and ugly. Girls' toys are more likely to be pastel in colour, bright, pretty and happy. 'Boy culture gets our dander up, but at least we accord it power and a certain amount of respect. But while Boy culture is demonised, Girl culture continues to be trivialised.'[11] The kind of things that girls and women seem to gravitate towards are: Barbie dolls, pretty clothes, make-up, 'soaps' and romances. All are usually dismissed in the media as trite or silly. Given the lack of respect accorded to the female domain in our culture, it is really not at all surprising that young boys are so eager to distance themselves from it. All of this has, I believe, major implications for education in general, and for religious education in particular, both at content and at process levels.

Competition has cropped up already in relation to the culture of the classroom. More generally, competitiveness is one of the characteristic motivators of our contemporary culture. It is to be seen at its best, or indeed worst, in the political, commercial and sporting worlds. (Is it also to be observed in ecclesiastical circles?) In school, teachers use it as a resource to motivate children to do all kinds of things, from learning tables and spellings to keeping the classroom tidy; from lining up, to behaving well. Most teachers employ competitiveness in minor or more extensive ways. One of the problems with this is that it ratifies the culture of competitiveness. It establishes a way of doing things which can lead to great pressure later on, particularly at examination times.

The all-pervasive nature of competition in our society indicates that it is one of the ways 'we do things 'round here'. When we talk about the ethos of a school, we usually think about Christian principles guiding the relationships between people in the school. I would suggest that an underlying principle in schools is more likely to be that of competitiveness. That influence can only increase with the introduction of national testing.

Competitiveness produces winners and, of course, losers. Everyone wants to win, no-one wants to lose. Conflicts arise. How are conflicts resolved ? Where do children learn to resolve conflicts? Perhaps most learning takes place at home, on the street, in school; however, they also learn about conflict in relationships from films and television. It should be noted that many of these film and television programmes, although deemed unsuitable, are often watched without parental knowledge or approval. Here, aggressiveness, physical contact and violence are the primary means by which conflicts are resolved. This is how many children, boys in particular, attempt to solve interpersonal conflicts. Walter Wink sees violence as 'the ethos of our times – the spirituality of the modern world.... Violence simply appears to be the nature of things. It is what works. It seems to be, the last and, often, the first resort in conflicts'.[12]

In addition, revenge, as a powerful motivator, is a very common theme in many of the films and television programmes which children watch. The general problem here is not that watching violent movies will generate a group of weapon-wielding psychopaths (though it will influence some) but that all of this exposure to the revenge/violence cycle desensitises children to violence and reduces their capacity for empathy, compassion and healing. One possible solution to this means of resolving conflict is training in impulse control. Daniel Goleman has urged this strongly:

> There is no psychological skill more fundamental than resisting impulse. It is the root of emotional self-control, since all emotions, by their very nature, lead to one or another impulse to act.... The capacity to impose a delay on an impulse is at the root of a plethora of efforts, from staying on a diet to pursuing a medical degree.[13]

However, in an era of instant gratification of needs and desires, this is going to be very difficult, especially for boys. Perhaps for too long, we have tended to shrug off boys' troublesome tendencies with a 'boys will be boys' attitude, when we really needed to listen very closely to what is going on for them. I'm reminded of a story that illustrates my point. A family settled down for dinner at the restaurant. The waitress first took orders from the adults, then turned to the seven-year-old. 'What will you have?' she asked. The boy looked around the table timidly and said 'I'd like a hot dog.' Before the waitress could write down the order, his mother interrupted. 'No hot dogs', she said. 'Get him a steak with mashed potatoes and carrots.' The waitress ignored her. 'Do you want ketchup or mustard on your hot dog?' she asked the boy. 'Ketchup', he replied. 'Coming up in a minute', said the waitress as she started for the kitchen. There was a stunned silence when she left. Finally, the boy looked at everyone present and said, 'She thinks I'm real!'

Because there are so many assumptions made about children, and so many demands made on them by parents, the media, teachers, peers, the State, industry, bishops/priests, and producers/advertisers, we need to pay attention to the lives and culture of children as they are.

One means of listening to children in a structured way is through research. In the context of this paper, it is interesting to note that there has been no major attempt in Ireland to publish research into primary school children's comprehension of religious language, concepts and images. Ronald Goldman conducted the last research in this area in England in the 1960s. While the lack of recent research is to be regretted, it is still possible to draw on personal experience to make some comments on the quality of religious education in our schools, and to make important connections between the experience of children and that of adults in this area. This is what I will do in the two short sections which will bring my remarks to a close.

Religion in education

As a subject in the curriculum religious education is a little like 'Gaeilge' – it thrives or falters on the significance it has at home or in the locality. It is common in urban schools to find that fewer than 25 per cent of children attend Sunday Mass regularly – not that Mass-going is the only measure of religious practice. However, for many children, it is the only contact they have with religion in their communities, outside of school. For them, religion's lack of any functional significance may go some way towards explaining the non-transfer of learning from the religious education lesson to behaviour in the yard.

An overall, planned programme of catechesis, therefore, needs to be directed towards adults in the community, not necessarily to help them help their children with their religious education programme but for the adults' own sake. Why do formal catechesis and religious education end at the completion of formal schooling? It seems strange that catechesis should be withdrawn with the greater part of the person's religious life ahead of them. As Walsh & Walsh pointed out over a decade ago:

> If the parents' faith rises little above that of children, they are in no position to provide an environment in which the religious understanding of the next generation can develop into an adult faith. There is an in-built limitation upon a child's opportunity for growth.[14]

There have been repeated calls for an improved and expanded adult religious education in recent decades, both internationally and here in Ireland. These have ranged from the Mulraney Conference in 1974, through *Catechesi Tradendae* (1976) and *Handing on the Faith,* to the most recent findings from dioceses all over the country in response to the research being conducted by Joe Dargan SJ in preparation for the formulation of a

National Pastoral Plan. Ten years ago, Bishop Donal Murray captured the urgency of this when he said:

> It is, however, now time for us in Ireland to take very seriously the statement of the General Catechetical Directory: 'Shepherds of souls should remember that catechesis for adults, since it deals with persons who are capable of an adherence that is fully responsible, must be considered the chief form of catechesis. All the other forms, which are indeed always necessary, are in some way oriented to it.' (n. 20)[15]

It is ironic, therefore, that these calls have been answered by the closures of Mount Oliver Institute, the Pastoral Department of The Dublin Institute of Adult Education, and the Galway Pastoral Centre, as well as the decline of the 'Tuesday night classes' organised through St Patrick's College, Maynooth.

Another problem in the context of religious education is not really one of catechesis, but of evangelisation. Or, at least, we are more likely to secure an effective or meaningful response if we pose the problem in this way. We cannot assume that children have heard the 'Good News'. Given that children form a sub-culture of their own, what is required here is a process of inculturation, not unlike that employed by missionaries, the basics of which are listening, dialogue and example/witness. The best place to undertake this is in the parish/community where the children live. This also offers children the opportunity to enrich their parish through their insights, questions and actions.

In tandem with such a community-based programme, religious education could also take place in school. We need to be clear about the motivation for doing this. We should organise religious education in schools, not because religious influence and religious practice are decreasing, but because values like co-operation, compassion and generosity are not supported by the predominant culture. We need religion now, not because Church structures and traditions are breaking down, but because social ties and moral norms are breaking down. Religious education has a place in the school, but only in so far as provision has already been made for it is the community.

Religious education – an aim for the future

Given that it is highly unlikely that religious education will be taken out of the hands of teachers for the foreseeable future, we need to consider what its inclusion in the school timetable aims to do. I believe we need to focus our attention on the creation of a programme of religious education, the purpose of which is, to quote Bishop Murray again,

> ...not to prepare unquestioning and compliant cogs for the smooth running of society as it is. It is to prepare people to be constructively critical, to take responsibility, to recognise the need for change. It is to give people a vision of human dignity and human purpose against which the shortcomings of any society can be judged and in the light of which something more human can be pursued.[16]

This will entail looking into the darkest recesses of 'the state we're in', as outlined above. It will also require faith and courage on the part of the educator. In this way we, along with our children, rather than simply being shaped by culture, can become shapers or architects of culture. Which brings me to my final story. This one concerns a woman who was a partner, a parent and a religious educator – someone who prayed a lot and who was involved in Earthwatch and her local Traveller Support Group. She had just been to a conference where one of the speakers had outlined the woes afflicting our society. She went home depressed. She cried out to God 'How is it that you, who loves us so much, can allow such things to happen? Why don't you do something?' Being a prayerful person, she waited through the long silence that followed. Then God answered her. 'I did', God said. 'I did do something – I made you.'

SECOND DISCUSSION

Chair: Anne Looney

Anne Looney: We have had three passionate presentations, if I may use that word, about religious education in the school. From Kieran Griffin, we heard about the fourth 'R', namely a religious education which emphasises rights, responsibilities and respect, but not excluding the possibility of religious instruction. Ann Walsh's presentation emphasised a religious education which asked the big questions of life and Tom Larkin has suggested to us the need for a religious education that might be involved in what he called 'reconstituting the world'. We can take just a few questions or comments at this point, but there will be more opportunities for questions and discussion during the symposium which follows the coffee break. So could we have the first contribution from the floor, please?

Paddy Kearns, religion teacher: This is a question about symbols. Many of the symbols which confront people today through advertising are very powerful ones, from Coca Cola to Manchester United. They have a deep influence on young people's attitudes and sometimes in a way which is worrying, leading to false perceptions of what is worthwhile in life. My question to the panel is: Have you come across any symbols which might be equally powerful and which might counteract some of the predominant influences of our present culture?

Anne Looney: Okay. Is there a second question which we might take to put with that?

Caroline O'Brien, religion teacher: My question is mainly for Ann Walsh. If we are to achieve all that we want to achieve as religious educators, the problem as I perceive it is that what we are giving them in schools is frequently at odds with the reality out there. The pupils, for instance, will see that the Church at parish and other levels is not in step with the religious education that they experience in school. So there's a problem for them when they go out into the world with ideals they want to believe in and find that the world is quite different. We would hope that they would struggle and be the people who would forge the future Church, but sometimes, due to the resistance they meet, they will ask 'what's the point?'

Anne Looney: We'll stay with these two questions for the moment. Kieran, would you like to address the first one about symbols?

Kieran Griffin: I acknowledge the power of symbols in our modern world. Indeed, as a parent, I'm acutely aware of this when I have to go and buy football jerseys for my children at inflated prices, not merely with the name of their favourite teams on them but also with the names of beers on them. I'm sure I'm not the only one present with this kind of experience. I think we have to look at symbols with children, be they the symbols of high-powered advertising or the models that are held up to them in school to help them interpret their own lives. The school that I'm in doesn't have icons, for the obvious reasons that things like crucifixes are offensive to some of the families who send their children to us. But all of the children in the school have to look at a whole range of symbols in our school's religious education programme. The chart I've displayed on the wall over here, for instance, contains important symbols from the world's different religions. I would suggest further that in a religious education programme not only is it important to explore religious symbols and their power, but also the influence of symbols in the non-religious sphere, such as advertising. I think children are very open to this kind of approach.

Anne Looney: The process of religious education you were proposing, Tom, included a critique of symbols, is that correct?

Tom Larkin: Yes, and here I want to take pursue further a point made by Michael Paul Gallagher last night when he quoted Michael Warren. I'm trying to emphasise the necessity of cultural analysis as part of our curriculum: to be able to look at what kinds of stories are being told to our children, or at who imagines our world for us. In looking at these kinds of questions in the context of the media, but not alone the media, we can better come to understand what it is they are trying to do to us. This provides young people with the choice of whether they want to go with this kind of manipulation or whether they want to reject it. Symbols are indeed powerful. Just yesterday, our entire country stopped for one minute in support of peace on the island of Ireland. That was a symbol of solidarity which sends a very powerful message. This white ribbon I'm wearing in my lapel is also a symbol of peace. If everyone is going around wearing one of these it's a statement that there is a huge community out there negating the forces of despair.

Ann Looney: I'm afraid we'll have to bring the discussion to an end here as I've been informed that we are running behind schedule. I'd like to thank our three speakers for the passion and conviction of their presentations. They have given us much food for thought this morning.

SYMPOSIUM
THE FUTURE OF RELIGION IN
IRISH EDUCATION

Chair: Dr Joseph Dunne

Panel: Rev Michael Drumm
Dr Michael Paul Gallagher SJ, Ann Walsh
Kieran Griffin, Tom Larkin

Dr Joseph Dunne: In this symposium we are keen to open the discussion to the floor and to give you, our participants, the opportunity to put questions and comments to panel members and to explore further some of the points raised by them in their presentations last night and this morning. I'm also conscious that there wasn't time to respond to all of the questions during the shortened discussion before the break, so perhaps we'll also get an opportunity to put that right during the symposium. As chairperson, I have been asked to set the ball rolling by picking out a few themes, or connections, or conflicts from the five presentations made. The idea here is not to pre-empt the discussion but to open it by identifying some common issues that have been raised and allowing participants from the floor and the panel to probe them further.

There are three things that have struck me. The first is the need, as I see it, for a more determinate specification of what we mean by religion. What has been at play a lot in several of the presentations is a very expansive and open definition of religion; not exactly a definition really, more an appeal for openness – of heart, of mind, of sensibility and so on. But if we take this route of openness in the sense suggested, how distinguishable then is religion from poetry or philosophy? Ann Walsh spoke of the teaching of religion in the context of the search for meaning. Tom Larkin spoke of it in the context of the breakdown of relationships and moral norms. It might be argued that subjects like philosophy, or ethics, or civic education, rather than religion, would be the appropriate ones here. So the question I'm raising is: What is the connection between religious education, in the sense of an open search for meaning and the transcendent and, on the other hand, religion as something rooted within a specific historical tradition – specifically a Christian or Catholic tradition? I was recently reading something by Flannery O'Connor, a great writer from the American South, where she made the point that nothing vaporises so quickly as religion, and particularly so when one talks about it as ultimate meaning and concern. She says that for her, religion has to be rooted in a particular tradition. I'd like if our speakers could clarify where they stand on this issue and, in doing this, show how the denominational, or the confessional aspects of religion stand in their considerations.

Turning now to the second issue on which we might focus, there has been a great emphasis placed on culture in the different presentations, perhaps even to the neglect of other forces in society, particularly economics, politics and the kinds of institutions that we have. The school is very much an institution, and therefore there is the whole question of power to be considered. My sense is that some of our speakers, indeed for very understandable reasons, have been keen to get away from the discourse of power and control which has bedevilled public debate on education because it has been so dominant. But I think there is something unsatisfactory in just putting this away, and having a more humane discourse here that we can all feel included in. I think there has to be some attempt to engage simultaneously with these two dimensions – what we might call the institutional-political on the one hand and the personal-spiritual on the other. And so that leads to the question of whether the school is the most appropriate arena for the kind of education in religion that has been spoken about during the course of the conference. You might like to pursue this in connection with the kind of questions Kieran Griffin raised: Should the school be an inclusive environment? Is this something that is required by the nature of a pluralist democracy? With political considerations like this in mind, would it be desirable not to have a denominational education in religion? Alternatively, bearing in mind the richness and the emancipatory import of what most of the panel had to say, the question might be asked: Is their understanding of religion a counter-cultural one? And, if so, is the school really the right arena for it? Can it co-exist with the dominant ethos of our schools at present, including the competitive and other pressures which reside there? This issue becomes more acute if we take into account the denominational aspects of religion, as this brings in the parish as a further arena, which hasn't come into focus in our deliberations at this conference. Michael Paul Gallagher spoke about the classroom and the retreat house, and it might be argued that whereas the logic of what he was saying was leading to something as unabashedly fervent as the retreat house, he still wanted to hold on to the classroom.

A final point that strikes me is that while we have had separate contributions on religion in primary, post-primary and third-level education, there might be more to be said on the continuities or discontinuities between them. I was struck last night by Val Rice's question about a Catholic university and also by Michael Drumm's answer, which was a robust 'no' to the desirability of a Catholic university in Ireland. In his answer you'll recall that Michael pointed out that unlike some other European countries, we don't, thankfully, have Catholic trade unions or Catholic farmers' associations. It struck me, however, that even though we don't have these kinds of Catholic associations, we do have Catholic schools. What logic, then, makes us think that a Catholic university is not a good idea, but that Catholic schools are? I'll open the discussion with these issues – to the panel, first, if they want to respond immediately, and, if not, then to participants from the floor.

Michael Drumm: Joe Dunne has raised a crucial point in his first issue, in that there are nuances in the way we are using the word 'religion' that have to be openly admitted. His suggestion is that if you were to draw your main conclusions from Tom Larkin's and Ann Walsh's presentations this morning and my own presentation last night, you might feel that religion can be summarised as a general search for meaning, as a transcendental form of openness. And of course there is a problem here from a philosophical point of view, because such a search can be addressed by a discipline called philosophy, or moral education, or indeed by the model of interdenominational education which Kieran Griffin detailed for us this morning.

Perhaps I didn't emphasise enough last night that I fully hold to the perspective that there is no such thing as religion outside of a tradition. It only exists within a concrete tradition. I don't recognise a notion of religion as just a general search for meaning. Of course it can be that, but only within one or more traditions. There is no such thing as a traditionless religion. For better or worse, religion always comes to us from within a tradition, and part of the business of the study of religion, particularly at third level, is to pursue its researches into tradition with a full acknowledgement that these researches themselves cannot escape tradition. Any kind of thinking that suggests that there can be some kind of escape from tradition, or some kind of independence of it, is avoiding the key difficult questions that have to be faced. Religion does come down to denominational questions in large part, and that is why there will always be disagreement between those who would hold that there can be a secular, non-confessional curriculum in religion, as outlined earlier this morning by Kieran Griffin, and, on the other hand, people like myself who believe that such a curriculum is not possible from a theological perspective. A curriculum can only operate, in my opinion, as a critical reflection on a particular tradition and then bring that tradition into dialogue with others. Religion exists only as lived in particular communities, as reflected on by those communities, and with all that ensues for better and for worse from that.

Tom Larkin: In relation to my remarks about children this morning, teachers are increasingly meeting children in classrooms who are, for all practical purposes, in a culture or sub-culture of their own. And if we take it that many of them haven't heard what I have called the Good News, then I think we need to look again at the question: How can you catechise such a group? I think you have to characterise the situation as a missionary one in the old sense of the word. One culture meets another one and that involves a long period of listening, of dialogue. It's going to place great demands on the religious educator. So in that sense, I believe that the idea of coming in with a well-worked out tradition is largely a non-starter for teachers' efforts with very many young people.

Kieran Griffin: I'd like to respond briefly to what Michael Drumm has said. Michael has described himself in his remarks last night and this morning as a theologian who works within a particular tradition. It is clear that in his work at third level he is also interested in dialogue with theologians from other traditions. Such discourse brings great benefits to the way people learn at third level. But if the definition of religion as pertaining to primary school is to be limited to one denominational tradition, and if religious education at this level is to be conceived as the handing on of this specific tradition, then the educational benefits of other perspectives are precluded from the classroom. This confronts us with the question: Is the primary school the proper place for this kind of activity to be carried on?

Michael Paul Gallagher: I think you have put your finger on something very important, Joe, in your comments on the tensions between different definitions of religion. I'd go even further and say this is even a tension within believers. To illustrate my point, let me refer briefly to differences between two noted theologians of our time, Hans Urs Von Balthasar and Karl Rahner, over how to reach people with the word of God in today's world. Simplifying for the sake of illustration, the Rahner approach is 'Listen to where people are'. The Balthasar approach is: 'God has spoken; isn't that the most important thing?' Now I think that as communicators, and particularly as educators, we have to live with that tension. And therefore the pastoral side of me, or the educational side of me, wants to do something like St Paul did on the Areopagus: 'I didn't like this Athens when I saw it first. It was trivial. It was stupid. But I have to respect their poetry. Indeed I have to talk to them in terms of their poetry or else they won't listen to me at all. And then I hope to get to mention Christ'. So there's a pedagogical, or initiation logic here which is very deep in the Church, and it does include religion as the search for meaning. And then there is the other logic that says: 'No, we are receivers of the word of God, and it is utterly concrete in Christ'. I think we see here two sides, not only in educational things but also in the spirituality of people who live in this moment.

Joseph Dunne: Thank you very much. Now, anybody from the floor, please?

Denis Bates, post-primary teacher: I'd like to put a general question and ask the panel to cast themselves in a prophetic role.

On the assumption that religion comes in as a subject at Leaving Certificate level, what could it bring to the system and the culture? If I might briefly state the worst case scenario, it would be that religion would become merely another examination subject, devoid of internal merit; a vehicle for points, no more, no less; simply a saddle for the rat in the rat race. But what could it be?

Joseph Dunne: Thank you. We can take one or two more questions before calling on the panel to respond.

Lily Mahon: This is something that was touched on by Tom Larkin. Maybe the focus should be on family and community religious education, rather than simply on the school. Children are already too separated from parents and grandparents and the wider community. They are continually being reminded that they have their own music, their own language, their own fashion. The wisdom of the elderly is not drawn upon, parents often find themselves floundering in their efforts to bridge different lifestyles. I think we urgently need to look at how religious education can involve all the family.

Roddy Day, primary teacher: I'd like to take up Joe Dunne's first question again, if I may. I know Michael Drumm dealt with it from a theological standpoint, but I'd like if Ann Walsh might address it from the standpoint of a post-primary teacher; in other words, if she'd say a few words on the distinction between a philosophical and a doctrinal conception of religion in the working context of the school. I'd like to address a question to Tom Larkin as well. I know very well from my own experience the kinds of difficulties you spoke about and I'd like if you would tell us something more about the strategies you developed to break down or overcome the kinds of resistance which met you efforts to teach religion. There's a third point I want to make. It's the Magisterium question which won't go away, no matter how much we attempt to place the emphasis on the more positive features of religion. In brief, the present pope, as far as I'm concerned, is an extremely conservative person. Maybe the battle to be fought in tackling the difficulties of religious education will have to be fought at that level as well.

Joseph Dunne: I can see there are many others with questions, but maybe we have enough on our plate for the moment to put to our panel.

Ann Walsh: I suppose I'd better take up the Leaving Certificate question first – the one raised by Denis Bates. The argument about religion as an examination subject in the Leaving Certificate has been with us in one form or another now for almost two decades. My own view is that examinations are no more the answer to the difficulties of religious education in the curriculum than they are the solution to any other educational question. Having said that, I'd like to add two comments. The first is that I'm not so sure about the realistic possibilities for education in the context of schooling unless some form of assessment and accountability are part of the picture. The idea of education without examinations is very attractive, but to be quite honest, attraction alone is not enough to sustain our human efforts and commitments in the long run. Only a minority of us are lovers of wisdom to such an extent that we need no external push. I recall from my own days as a student in Mater Dei, for all my genuine interest in theology, the discipline imposed by examinations made me read and study a lot more than I otherwise would have done. Secondly, and coming specifically now to the proposals that the NCCA have brought forward, not only have they proposed a course of studies in religion for the Leaving Certificate, but they have also proposed one for the Junior Certificate. It is to be included among the options for the

Leaving Certificate, and I feel that only a minority will take it for the exam, but many more may take the Junior Certificate exam, and I am much more interested in the educational possibilities at this level, where the exam is not attended by the competitive pressure for points. Now if these possibilities are not availed of to render our pupils theologically more literate in general, then I'm in agreement with your worst case scenario. But herein lies the challenge for us and I'd like to try it, because we haven't tried it to date. The nature and orientation of the course itself, and of the examination format that is devised, should help to remove obstacles of all sorts which have been accumulating over the years.

Joseph Dunne: Would you like to take Roddy Day's question as well, now that you have the floor?

Ann Walsh: Yes. As you were articulating this question in your own introduction, Joe, and again as Roddy was voicing it in the context of the classroom just now, I found myself thinking 'Can we not even live long enough with a philosophical question before we are overcome by the difficulties with it? The doctrinal concept of religion is familiar to us. It involves the transmission of a body of knowledge, a set of answers. But it is my belief that we haven't lived with the search long enough. We haven't lived with it in education; most of us haven't lived with it in our lives. We tend to be in too much of a rush to find the denominational angle, the doctrinal angle, so as to close the question. The ideal is a correlation between the philosophical question and the doctrinal response. The search is not the final step. I'm very much in agreement with Michael Paul Gallagher when he quotes Rahner on the issue which is really the ultimate one raised by this question: 'I don't believe in God because I have worked everything out to the satisfaction of my mind. I continue to believe in God because I pray every day'. At the end of the day there does come a challenge of this kind, the challenge of a leap of faith. Clearly then, it's not the challenge of a seductive religion that makes me feel good. It's more the challenge of a disturbing kind of religion that may not make me feel good about the kind of lifestyle I'm leading, or whatever. I think it's important, then, to be able to live with the question in an engaged and active way, particularly if we are teachers. This is the kind of openness I have in mind, not a vague, feel-good kind of openness. And far from something which vaporises quickly, it requires a commitment and conviction which goes well beyond that called for by orthodoxy in a given tradition.

Joseph Dunne: Thank you, Ann. Perhaps you'd like to respond, Tom, to the question about the strategies you use to overcome resistances you've met in teaching religion in the primary school?

Tom Larkin: Yes, This is something I didn't get around to looking at in my presentation. In relation to the boy/girl cultures, the issue of role models is at the heart of it. I think it's important to offer children real role models; to offer girls, in particular, models of really strong women who can take charge of their lives, who can do things. These would be models that boys can look up to as well as girls. In this regard, one of the problems with our religious education programme is the rather colourless representation of Jesus in some of the textbooks, and I don't just mean the pastel colours and toyshop colours used in the books. I was thinking about this in class one day while trying to get the pupils' images of Jesus. The terms the pupils were using to describe Jesus were 'love', 'care', 'share', and so on, and then I threw in the question: 'Is Jesus a wimp?' And the reaction from the class was: 'No, he's not'. So I pushed the issue further and asked them if they could see a strong Jesus anywhere in the stories we were following in the text; for instance the Jesus who was really strong with Pilate? the Jesus who got angry and threw the moneylenders out of the Temple? I feel that this Jesus is largely absent from the religious education programmes in the primary schools.

So the strategy there is to present a role model worthy of the pupils' real commitments. Another strategy is to teach the children the value of silence, particularly as they are surrounded by noise most of the time. My purpose here is to try to offer the pupils an opportunity to meet with God in their own space. They really crave this, whether or not they go to Mass or are otherwise interested in religious observances. Combining this kind of approach with the use of strong role models can lead to children acting for justice in the world. I believe that this combination of action and reflection can inspire them in the longer term.

Joseph Dunne: We'll go back to the floor now for some further questions.

Fiachra Long, University College Cork: I would like to echo the first question Joe Dunne mentioned, and I fear that I may be running against the tide in asking about the notion of search. I know that the notion of search has a very long theological tradition, and we remember those beautiful words of Augustine: 'Our hearts are ever restless Lord, until they rest in thee'. We can find plenty of texts that corroborate the view that a religious view of life is a search. However, against that, if we look at what a number of speakers here have been describing as the cultural conditions of believers today, or of non-believers, or of the indifferent, it seems to be insufficient to say something like 'scratch the surface a little bit, and there you will find, in pristine condition, a fundamental search for meaning, or God, or whatever'. It seems to me that one of the problems of the spiritual condition when it gets to an advanced stage of decay is that, scratch as you will, you won't get back to this kind of pristine search for God. So it worries me a bit that any programme for religious education, as an exam subject or otherwise, should be predicated on a search for meaning, as if this were a transparent condition for everyone.

Joseph Dunne: Anybody else?

Caroline O'Brien, religion teacher: I'd like to come back to the question I put at the discussion session earlier this morning but which wasn't addressed at that stage because we ran out of time. My question is: If I educate my pupils sincerely in their religion, where is their future, particularly in a world where there is little out there for them in the world at large which would sustain them and enable them to continue that education as adults? It seems to me, then, that there is a great need to develop links between school and parish, because your education doesn't stop, or shouldn't stop, when you leave school. I think we need to put plans in place to enable people's religious education to continue after they leave school, so there is a major role here for the parish.

Joseph Dunne: We'll take one more question before returning to the panel.

Tony McCarthy, religion teacher: I have a difficulty with the turn the discussion here is taking. The difficulty I have is in relying on concepts like parish, and in calling for support structures for religious education in the community – ones that are primarily denominational in character, or that no longer meet the needs of many people, including myself, in terms of their personal search. There is a presumption here that such structures are the ones which will facilitate the religious sense of belonging amongst young people once they leave school. When I hear this I feel a sense of suffocation, of having my breathing system closed down as it were, whereas for most of the conference my sense was the opposite one of a refreshing opening up. I feel that when most pupils come into second-level schools from primary school they are really open to religion, but by the time they come to leave second level, so many of them have become closed, or alienated. So there is a need, particularly at this level, to hold back on ready-made answers and to go down the road of searching. I don't think there are too many ready-made answers that will serve the future.

Joseph Dunne: Let's put these questions to the panel for response now before coming back to the floor again.

Michael Drumm: The tension is there all the time between religion as institution and religion as personal search, and the questions and comments are returning to this issue in different ways. But when we look at the issue critically, and acknowledge that the school is the place where formal religious education takes place, we have to admit that the school is the most institutionalised set-up of all. The educational system is more institutionalised than religion. In religion, moreover, there are other pathways you can take and you can avoid the worst elements of institutionalisation if you want. There is no way, until you are at least sixteen years of age, that you can avoid the institutionalisation of school. Schooling is the most tyrannical system of all, it leaves religion in the shade, and that has to be admitted. At its best, religion sows the seeds of freedom and hope. At its worst, it is deadly and poisonous and sectarian. And as Michael Paul Gallagher has illustrated, these two extremes exist in most communities and in society at a global level. But the crux of the matter is religion in the school. And because the school as an institution has historically tended to be a dictatorship, you can get the worst forms of religion in the school. When you think of the Magisterium's perspective in this – the Magisterium is the bishops, not the clergy or other believers

– there's not a member of the Magisterium anywhere in the world who would not agree that the search for meaning is the most wonderful search you could embark upon, and they would probably go a long way down that road with you. But where religious education is concerned, the search for meaning occurs very largely within a school context, not outside of it, and that's where the question of links between the institutional Churches and the State schools comes up as a problematic question.

But one last word on this. There's one hope for the future of the Church in Irish society that's highlighted here this weekend. And that is that theology has become de-clericalised, a great move forward that has happened without being planned by anybody. Nobody can stop that. In fairness, the Magisterium, in its Irish manifestation, facilitated this and should be applauded for it. It was institutions like Mater Dei and Maynooth and others that provided the possibility – without State funding – for the broadening and flourishing of theology as a field of study. And now that people who have come through these institutions are in a position to take over leadership roles, we have moved beyond the clericalisation of theology in religious thinking. That in itself will give us a new language and a new way of understanding institutional links. A priest, or a member of a religious order working in a school, clearly has very tight institutional links with the school and with the Church. Obviously, lay people will have a much freer role in the schooling situation and their ideas, as we can already see at this conference, will sow great seeds of renewal. These will push forth the boundaries of religion, and of our understanding of it. Whether they change the nature of the school as an institution is a bigger question.

Tom Larkin: There are three questions before us that are similar to each other, which I'd like to address: Tony McCarthy's, Caroline O'Brien's and an earlier one (Lily Mahon, p. 114) on religious education and family life. It is interesting to note that twenty years ago the Catholic bishops decided at a conference in Kerry that adult religious education was going to be a priority. In 1979 the papal encyclical, *Catechesi Tradendae,* said that the parish must become the prime place and pre-eminent mover of catechesis. In their publication *Handing on the Faith,* the Irish bishops reiterated the message that the adults in a community are the ones who need to be the focus of catechesis. A Jesuit priest, Fr Joe Dargan, was commissioned by the bishops to help them develop a national pastoral plan. He met with most of the bishops around the country and noted that one of the top priorities for them was the need for adult religious education. While he was going around from diocese to diocese, the Institute of Religious Education in Mount Oliver, Dundalk, one of the country's chief centres for educating adult religious educators, was closed down. The Dublin Institute for Adult Education, a major centre for training people in pastoral ministry, was closed down. The Galway Pastoral Centre was closed down. The adult religious education component of the Diploma in Adult and Community Education at Maynooth was removed. So, on the one hand, there are all the calls for adult religious education, and on the other, the very structures to promote it are actually being closed down. So I'm left wondering: what are they afraid of? I have to ask that question. Members of a mature community are going to ask questions in any case, and will have to live with questions. When people take their faith journey seriously, they will be asking questions all the time. Learning to live with questions is something we must be able to do, but it is a challenge.

Michael Paul Gallagher: I'm still struck by Ann Walsh's first contrast – between pupils' indifference to the video on humanism and their avid interest in the artist talking about his work on religious themes. This contrast calls to my mind a quotation from a Scripture scholar called Mollat talking about faith in the Gospel of St John. He says 'Faith, in St John, is a matter of the quality of looking'. It's a word that we haven't been using – quality. I think religious education has everything to do with what that artist achieved with the pupils. He opened a wavelength, which wasn't just a matter of searching. It could be more than searching. It could be a sense that God is close. You'll recall the film *Dead Poets' Society.* Yes, it was naive, but its heart was in the right place. It's as if in the communication of religion, perhaps particularly in Ireland, there is a suppressed but strong poetry.

I might make two quick remarks on a few of the questions before us: first in relation to the question of 'out there', or 'how does our religious education prepare pupils for out there?' I don't have an answer. I have an addition: It's not just the parish, it's the parents. I'm wondering about the messages they are getting from the parents as well as the boredom they are getting from the parish. My hunch is that the school and the religion teacher may have a great service to offer to awakening hope in the parents; that they could grow, that they wouldn't abdicate and throw the sponge in your direction. I think that's a key issue.

That would also be my line of response to the question about what religious education could be, as distinct from just another examination subject, Denis Bates' question. Viewed from a positive viewpoint, I would say that religion could get a respectability that would give people tools for hope for the future. In other words if they see that this subject has an intellectual coherence and is taken seriously in the curriculum, they might conclude 'Ah, there's more in it than I thought'. That's not to say that all would thereby become believers, but that pupils would be left with tools for hope for when they leave schools; that they would be aware that there's more to religion than something that can be simply dismissed because they don't like one or other aspect of it.

Joseph Dunne: I know that other members of the panel would like to respond to some of the questions that are already before us, but there are quite a few in the audience who have signalled their desire to ask questions or make contributions, and as time is now slipping by I'll take some more contributions from the floor at this stage

Unidentified religion teacher: One of the themes that struck me, certainly in three of the papers, probably in all five, was the question of language, and the search for a language. Last night Michael Paul Gallagher suggested that in cultures where unbelief has become common the language of religion is somehow foreign to human experience. Michael Drumm remarked that one of the challenges for theologians was to find a public language in which to speak of private things. This morning Ann Walsh quoted a poet, a priest, and in doing so she likened those of us who are religious educators to people who belong 'out by the side of things'; we have a story to tell, 'but when we open our mouths, no words take shape'. Finding a language in which we can communicate with the worlds of our students is a great challenge for us. I would be worried, however, if, in taking up this challenge, we allow that language to be sourced somewhere other than in the cultures and sub-cultures of our students. In particular I'm worried that a rather secular and academic religious education will bring with it a language and examination requirements which are alien ones. I would suggest that examinations in themselves are already a language that alienates very many of our students. I'd be uneasy about bringing religious education down the road of examinations without some serious further consideration

Secondly, we often forget that language itself is culturally rooted, and when we come to search for a language that we can share with our students, it's not enough to identify that in their culture with which we can speak. We must also be open to changing our own language, and being changed ourselves by it.

Joseph Dunne: There is a further question here.

Second unidentified religion teacher: Michael Paul Gallagher spoke about the quality of looking. I want to take up this idea of quality in the context of listening to our students. I consider myself a religious educator and I'm there to listen to my students and to educate them about religion in all its aspects. I'm wondering if there has been much research done on asking students what they want. I'm aware of a study carried out about two years ago by students in a Limerick school, where they went around asking other students what they thought about religion, about the methodologies used to teach it and so on. When they brought their results to the bishop they weren't heard. They entered their project in the Young Scientist competition and they got an award for it. The students' project was focusing on this issue of quality in religious education. It's quality that our students are looking for, and as religious educators we need to be much more aware of this and to follow up with work in the schools.

Joseph Dunne: So, it's back to the panel for the final response.

Ann Walsh: Underlying many of the observations and questions here this morning is something akin to the difference between, on the one hand, religious education as functional, and on the other, religious education as liberating. As responses from the panel have already pointed out, there may be an ever-recurring tension between these two emphases. But perhaps I can indicate something more of my own thinking on the matter, firstly by agreeing with the point made by the last speaker. The starting-point must be one of listening to the pupils. But I would go further and say that the experience of the pupils there and then has to be deepened and broadened to a point where it can be shared. I'm not happy with appealing to a transitory teenage experience that's soon gone, one that they are almost embarrassed about as soon as they have gone through a particular phase of growing up. I'm more convinced that no matter what age you are, you can sufficiently deepen an experience to a point where it can be shared, not just by other people at that time, but where it can be shared culturally and in a tradition. This is where Michael Drumm's remarks on religion in tradition are particularly pertinent.

Relating this briefly to some of the other questions, if religion is to serve any educational purpose in the mainstream of curriculum and examinations, it's about pushing people beyond the horizons of, say, 'my little world here and now', or 'my set of concerns', or 'my symbols'; because, valuable and all as these are, they will fade too, and they will be replaced. So, in a longer view, religion in the curriculum, its language and its symbols, is about pushing those horizons and concerns beyond transitory ones to something which resonates in everybody, in every culture. And this brings me to the suggestion (Fiachra Long's) that no matter how much you may scratch beneath the surface with some people, you will not find a search for meaning, yearning to be engaged. I have some sympathy with this suggestion and I acknowledge that there can be a certain arrogance in presuming that this sense of search must be there. However I would like to test the assumption underlying this suggestion – in other words to really 'scratch the surface' not just a little bit but a lot, and find out what is there. I'm not so sure that we have done that in recent years in religious education. And until we have it is difficult either to agree or to disagree with the suggestion.

Joseph Dunne: Ann has the last word from the panel. I'd like to thank our five speakers, you, our participants, for your attendance, your attention and your contributions, Anne Marie Kieran who brought the roving microphone to individual contributors from the floor of this amphitheatre, so that your contributions could be recorded for publication purposes. And finally I'd like very much like to thank the organising committee for the conference, those who conceived the idea and planned the programme. Those were Pádraig Hogan and Kevin Williams of the Educational Studies Association of Ireland, with some help from Fr Donal Harrington and Padraig Conway of the Irish Theological Association and Robert Dunne of the Religion Teachers' Association. So, our thanks to all of those.

AFTERWORD
THE EXPANDING HORIZONS OF CATHOLIC EDUCATION

Dermot A. Lane

To be rooted is perhaps the most important and least recognised need of the human soul. It is one of the hardest to define. A human being has roots by virtue of his real, active, and natural participation in the life of a community, which preserves in living space certain particular treasures of the past and certain particular expectations for the future.[1]

The organisers of the conference on 'The Future of Religion in Irish Education' held in St Patrick's College, Drumcondra, February 1996 are to be congratulated for providing a most successful forum of constructive educational exchange. The quality of the papers presented and the level of participation in the plenary sessions augurs well for the future of education in Ireland. The openness and civility of the conversations conducted throughout the weekend were an instructive model of the value of pluralism within educational discourse. The actual publication of the proceedings is an added bonus for the participants as well as a real service to the wider educational public.

I am grateful to the editors of the proceedings for the invitation to offer an 'Afterword' to the conference. Instead of summarising the wealth of discussion at the conference I have decided to address one particular issue that was hovering around the edges of debate at the conference, namely the expanding horizons of Catholic education.

Criticism of Catholic education

The public profile of Catholic education, especially as found in Church-run schools and their programmes of religious education, is the subject of much criticism in Ireland today by the media, teachers' unions, some teachers, and a few politicians. It would be obscurantist simply to dismiss this criticism as just another example of gratuitous Church-bashing. Some of the criticism is surely justified but, equally, some of it is ill-informed and often targeted at a Church belonging to bygone days. Further, it is unfortunate that much of this criticism is directed at issues related to the apparent power and control of education by the Catholic Church in Ireland. While legal discussions about the ownership of schools, the composition of Boards of Management, and the number of trustee representatives on boards have their place, they should not be allowed to detract from the educational self-understanding of the Church.

The Catholic Church is involved in schooling and Religious Education because it is committed to the holistic development of pupils in a way that embraces the physical, intellectual, affective, aesthetic, spiritual, moral, religious and Christian development of the individual. The primacy of the Church's commitment to this development of the whole person can be found in a variety of sources: the documents of Vatican II, the Catholic social teaching of the Church, and various Church statements on education since the Council. Rarely, if ever, does criticism of the Catholic Church's involvement in education address this body of literature and its vision of holistic development. Instead criticism is directed against what I would call a post-Tridentine experience and understanding of Catholicism as manifested in Catholic schools and programmes of religious education prior to Vatican II.

The Catholic Church has expanded the horizons of its own self-understanding since Vatican II, and these enlarged horizons have far-reaching implications for the organisation of Catholic schools and their programmes of religious education.

Prior to Vatican II this post-Reformation Catholicism described itself over against the Protestant Reformation, existing in opposition to the modern world as shaped by the spirit of the Enlightenment, and having little regard for the major religions of the world. This Counter-Reformation Church was defensive, exclusivist, and introverted. This Church flourished in Ireland, and elsewhere, up to the mid-1960s. It found expression in claims like 'outside the Church, there is no salvation' and 'error has no rights'.

The impact of Vatican II on Catholic education

At Vatican II a significant change took place in the self-understanding of Catholicism. Some would describe the change as a development in doctrine, others saw it as a new Pentecost, and still others perceived it as a reformation – something we can leave to the judgement of church historians. At the very least it involved an expansion of horizons which the Church is still coming to grips with – especially in the area of education.

This expansion of horizons brought about a new openness between the Church and the modern world. From then on the Church seeks to be in conversation, dialogue and solidarity with the modern world.[2] While the Church claims to have something to offer to the modern world it also acknowledges that it has something to learn from the modern world – even to the extent of admitting that it has 'greatly profited ... from the antagonism of those who oppose or persecute her'.[3]

Further, the expansion of horizons at Vatican II saw the Church, in its decree on ecumenism, affirm the ecclesial reality of other Christian Churches and acknowledge that they contain 'a certain, though imperfect, communion with ... the Catholic Church'.[4] Division among Christian Churches, it is pointed out, 'openly contradicts the will of Christ, provides a stumbling-block to the world and inflicts damages on ... the cause of proclaiming the good news'.[5] The Catholic Church admits that blame for these divisions belongs to 'both sides'[6] and that therefore the Catholic Church is summoned by Christ 'to that continual reformation of which she always has needs'.[7]

In addition, this widening of horizons embraces what is often referred to as the challenge of inter-Faith dialogue, namely the call to enter into dialogue with members of non-Christian religious communities.[8] The Council recognises that other religions can prepare the way for the acceptance of the truth of the Gospel to which all Christians must bear witness.[9] In particular the Council teaches that world religions such as Islam, Hinduism, Budhism and Judaism 'often reflect a ray of that truth which enlightens all' and that the Church 'rejects nothing which is true and holy in these religions'.[10]

These three examples of the expanded self-understanding of the Catholic Church that took place at Vatican II are endorsed in subsequent synods (e.g. the 1985 extraordinary Synod of Bishops, Rome) and Church statements; they have far-reaching implications for the way one organises, structures and understands the Catholic school and its programmes of religious education today.

It means, for example, that the Catholic school must be open to the modern world and modern culture – no longer being inward-looking or exclusivist. Consequently the Catholic school must be in critical dialogue with modern culture, affirming what is positive about modernity in terms of democratic principles, human rights and the struggle for social justice, while at the same time negating the destructive dimensions of modernity such as excessive individualism, a market-led capitalism, and the exploitation of nature. Above all the Catholic school must be able to talk meaningfully and imaginatively about the mystery of God in the face of modernity and the emerging strands of post-modernity – not by pushing God out to the margins but, as some of the great Christian thinkers down through the centuries have insisted, as present in all things.

Further, the Catholic school must be a centre committed to the promotion of ecumenical dialogue among all Christian Churches 'not (as) … some sort of "appendix" which is added to the Church's traditional activity', but as 'an organic part of her life and work, and consequently must pervade all that she is and does'.[11] In making this commitment to ecumenism Vatican II urges Catholics not just to wait but to take initiatives in advancing Christian unity.[12]

In addition, the Catholic school, in the light of Vatican II, must also respect and be seen to respect the values of other world religions as well as being ready to enter into dialogue with members of non-Christian religions. It was therefore disappointing to find some voices recently objecting to proposals for the study of world religions put forward by the National Council for Curriculum and Assessment in its draft syllabi for religious education. These expanded horizons of Catholic identity must surely be incorporated into the way we express and implement the ethos obtaining in Catholic schools. In particular these enlarged perspectives will permeate religious education programmes in Catholic schools.

This new self-understanding of Catholicism at Vatican II, and, by implication, of what constitutes a Catholic school, is premised on a humble awareness by the Church of its own need for internal reform and renewal. A central element within this renewal of the Church and her schools is the conversion that will come about through contact with other Christian Churches and through inter-Faith dialogue. Perhaps even more important is the fact that this inclusive understanding of Catholicism and the Catholic school recovers something of the original pre-Reformation meaning of what it meant to be Catholic.

The denominational question

If the Catholic school and religious education are of their nature in the light of Vatican II, committed to inter-Church and Inter-Faith-Dialogue, where does that leave the denominational character of Catholic education? Is there any further need for denominational education? Why not at least integrate all the Christian denominations into one new reality? These particular questions capture something of the current 'politically correct' thinking about denominational education. It is a view, however well-intentioned, that totally misunderstands the dynamism of ecumenism, the nature of Christianity, and the reality of Church history.

Ecumenism is not about putting together the lowest common denominator among the Christian Churches, nor is it a blending together of differences. Instead ecumenism is about the shared quest among individual Christian Churches for what some call 'full visible unity among all baptised', or others describe as the possibility of 'reconciled diversity' or 'conciliar fellowship' among the Christian denominations. The goal of ecumenism will only come about through the internal reform and renewal of the different Christian Churches. Ecumenism presupposes denominational identity as a point of departure on the way to Christian unity. Without an owning of denominational Christian identity there will be no internal reform and renewal of individual Churches, nor can there be any real appreciation of the richness and difference of the other Christian denominations.

Dr Robin Eames, the Church of Ireland Archbishop of Armagh, is surely right in his Presidential address to the General Synod of the Church of Ireland in May 1996 when he says that 'Ecumenism must never be allowed become a sort of new denomination. The real ecumenist is one who knows and accepts the ethos of his or her own Church and from that position of strength reaches out to fellow Christians in charity and understanding.'[13]

Further, it must be pointed out that, theologically speaking, there is no such thing as Christianity in the abstract. The Christian reality only exists as mediated by particular traditions and historical ecclesial communities. Christianity is more than just an interesting idea; it is a particular praxis embodied in living communities of people unified by Christian faith, worship and organisation.

An important moment in ecumenical dialogue is the healing of memories. However, before the transformation of memories can take place we need to hear about our mutually alienating historical memories. To pretend that ecclesial divisions do not exist, or to deny the presence of ecclesial differences, is to misrepresent the Christian reality and unwittingly to anaesthetise the pain of separation that is an integral part of the engine of ecumenism in the quest for unity.

This particular perception of the importance of denominational education, recognised by most of the Christian Churches, is underpinned by contemporary hermeneutical theory. Genuine dialogue, whether with experience, an event, a text, or a Christian denomination, takes place from within a particular historical perspective, social location and cultural bias. It is out of this complex amalgam of 'prejudice' that appreciation of the other and of difference takes place. It is also out of this particular personal perspective that we can critique the tradition that has shaped our identity. Every human being has roots and these roots are the very foundation of dialogue as well as the possibilty of their transformation in the future. There are no neutral, or value-free, or pure vantage points in education or religion from which we can encounter the other.

Even contemporary philosophy of science recognises that the idea of the detached observer is dead and that the scientist in the pursuit of so-called scientific objectivity is always subjectively engaged. The relativity theory and quantum mechanics reveal that the position of the observer influences the shape of the observed. It would surely be ironic if education or religion began to adopt the so-called scientific hypotheses of detachment and neutrality when science itself and hermeneutical theory are proclaiming the defects of such an understanding of knowledge and interpretation.

Non-denominational religious education, as distinct from non-denominational education, runs the risk of denying the scandal and pain of division among the Christian Churches which drives the ecumenical movement. Likewise, non-denominational Christian education distorts history and ignores the sociology of Christianity. On the other hand, it must be acknowledged that in the past denominational Christian education may have given rise to sectarian attitudes. Consequently, any defence or promotion of denominational education must take account of this particular danger.

There is considerable confusion at present about a linkage between denominational education and sectarianism. In the minds of some, denominational education and sectarianism are synonymous. It is not uncommon to find otherwise well-informed journalists moving directly from discussions about Catholic education to charges of sectarianism. Such claims may have been justified in the past, especially in the light of the Protestant Reformation and the movement of a counter-Reformation style of Catholicism which has persisted right up to the middle of this century. However, since the formation of the World Council of Churches in 1948 and the event of Vatican II in the mid-1960s, such charges can hardly be justified – given the declared ecumenical intentions of the mainline Christian Churches today. It needs to be said that the promotion or, indeed, toleration of sectarian attitudes in a Catholic school is explicitly at variance with the teaching of the Catholic Church. This does not mean, however, that the Vatican II vision of Catholic education is always in place and operative on the ground; instead this vision must be continuously cultivated and renewed.

The shadow of sectarianism must confront all the Christian Churches in Ireland today and challenge them in their denominational education to live up to their respective ecumenical commitments. It is far from clear, however, that sectarianism will be eliminated by blurring the denominational differences or pretending that they do not exist. Instead it seems more likely, for the reasons outlined above, that sectarianism will be better overcome by a denominational education that is explicitly and formally ecumenical. Without this ecumenical dimension denominational education runs the risk of engendering sectarian attitudes. Consequently the ecumenical commitment ought to be formally inscribed into the mission statements and religious education programmes of Catholic schools today. It is this commitment to ecumenical dialogue within denominational education that will effect the much needed internal reform and renewal of denominational identity.

One further point that arises out of denominational education is the issue of pluralism. Again there are some who herald pluralism triumphantly as the end of denominational education. Pluralism is promoted in some circles in direct contrast to and contradiction of denominational identity. The issue here is as much one about the meaning of pluralism as it is about denominational education. Surely pluralism must be distinguished from relativism, which is indifferent to the integrity of all other points of view, including denominational education.

Yet the question must be faced: Is denominational education compatible with the pluralism emerging in the new Ireland? Genuine pluralism, in contrast to a lazy pluralism, is about the valuation of differences and giving them space in the public forum. Pluralism is not about a levelling out of distinctiveness but rather a celebration of difference in such a way that all participants in the conversation can benefit from the encounter with the otherness of each other.

From a Catholic point of view this means recognising, as Vatican II did through its Decree on Religious Freedom, that pluralism in public life must be valued and respected. Likewise the Council recognised that pluralism in the life of the Church is something to be fostered in a spirit of 'mutual esteem, reverence, and harmony'.[14] The guiding principle in the face of pluralism, whether in the public forum or in the life of the Church, should be that ancient insight reiterated at Vatican II: 'let there be unity in what is necessary, freedom in what is unsettled, and charity in every thing else'.[15]

The Catholic Church, therefore, should welcome the development of other, alternative forms of educational choice such as the Gaelscoileanna, multi-denominational education, and non-denominational education. This does not necessarily mean that the Church has to accept the underlying philosophy of such alternatives, but rather that it respects their existence. Such diversity of form and choice in education can only be good for Catholic education as it will act as a stimulus to develop what is distinctive about its own identity and ethos. The absence of diversity in education in the past has not always served the best interests of Catholic education.

To conclude this note on the expanding horizons of Catholic education it is important to emphasise that these new vistas of Vatican II should be incorporated into the ethos, structures and curriculum of Catholic schools. The Catholic school of the future ought to be distinctive in its critical openness to the modern and post-modern world, prominent in promoting ecumenical activity, and active in the embrace of inter-Faith dialogue. The advent of religious education as an examination subject in the near future and the publication of the 1997 Education Bill present Catholic schools with a new opportunity – indeed a *kairos* – to rediscover the real meaning of being Catholic, which includes, among other things, the fostering of unity in the midst of diversity.

NOTES

Foreword

1. The presentations by various representative bodies to the National Education Convention have been kept on record and bound in two volumes by the Secretariat of the National Education Convention. Those by the religious bodies appear in *Presentations to the National Education Convention – Part One* (Dublin: National Education Convention Secretariat, 1994). A list of the many recent publications of the CMRS/CORI on educational issues is available from the CORI Education Office, Milltown Park, Dublin 6.

Chapter 1: Religion in Irish Education: Recent Trends in Government Policy

1. Government of Ireland, *Education for A Changing World:* Green Paper on Education (Dublin: The Stationery Office, 1992). Government of Ireland, *Charting our Education Future:* White Paper on Education (Dublin: The Stationery Office, 1995).

   Some of the arguments in this chapter are raised in another context in an article entitled 'Religious Education and State Policy in Ireland', *Panorama,* Vol. 7. No. 1 (summer, 1995), which I wrote in collaboration with my colleague, Andrew McGrady. I am grateful to him and to Fiona Williams for helping me to clarify my thinking on the issues as they are presented here.

2. *Education for A Changing World,* op. cit., pp. 33 and 87.
3. Ibid., p. 33; *Charting Our Education Future,* op. cit., p. 10.
4. *Education for A Changing World,* op. cit., p. 96.
5. *Charting Our Education Future,* op. cit., pp. 47/48.
6. Ibid., pp. 48/49.
7. Ibid., p. 52.

8. *Education for A Changing World,* op. cit., p. 90.

9. Ibid., pp. 90/91.

10. The Convention Secretariat, John Coolahan (Ed.) *Report on the National Education Convention* (Dublin: The Stationery Office, 1994), p. 33.

11. *Charting Our Education Future,* op. cit., p. 23.

12. Ibid.

13. Ibid.

14. Ibid., pp. 23/24.

15. Ibid., p. 217.

16. Ibid., p. 24.

17. *Education for A Changing World,* op. cit., p. 129; *Charting Our Education Future,* op. cit., p. 156.

18. *Education for A Changing World,* op. cit., pp. 13, 130-131.

19. Ibid. p. 129; *Charting Our Education Future,* op. cit., p. 161.

20. Department of Education, Circular Letter M4/95 (Dublin, 1995).

21. Ibid.

22. Ibid.

23. National Council for Curriculum and Assessment, *Civic, Social and Political Education at Post-Primary Level* (Dublin: The Stationery Office, 1993).

24. In Kevin Williams, 'Public Examinations and Religious Education', *The Furrow,* Vol 46, no. 7/8 (1995), and in a reply to a response to my article by Dominic Johnson OSB in *The Furrow,* vol. 46. no.11 (1995), pp. 656-659, I develop the arguments raised here.

25. See the response by Dominic Johnson OSB in *The Furrow,* Vol.46, No.11 (1995) pp. 655-656, and 'Public Examinations and Religious Education' by Martin Convey in the same issue.

Chapter 2: New Forms of Cultural Unbelief

1. Raymond Williams, 'Culture is Ordinary', reprinted in

Studying Culture: An Introductory Reader Ann Gray and Jim McGuigan (eds.) (London: Edward Arnold, 1993), pp.5-14. Quotation from p.6.

2. Josef Vives, 'Dios en el crepusculo del siglo XX' *Razon y Fe* (Mayo 1991), p.468. (My translation)

3. As this paper was going to press I read Donal Dorr's recent book entitled *Divine Energy* (Dublin: Gill & Macmillan, 1996). It offers a lively defence of certain New Age sensibilities and healthily warns against mere condemnation of this spiritual phenomenon.

4. William Barry, 'US Culture and Contemporary Spirituality', *Review for Religious,* Vol. 54, January-February 1995, p. 7.

5. J. H. Newman, *Grammar of Assent* (London: Longman, 1901) pp. 92-93.

6. T. S. Eliot, *On Poetry and Poets* (London: Faber & Faber, 1957), p. 25.

7. Alain Touraine, *Critique of Modernity,* trans. D. Macey (Oxford: Blackwell, 1995), pp. 295, 370.

8. Michael Warren, *Communications and Cultural Analysis* (Westport, Connecticut: Bergin & Garvey, 1992), p. 118.

9. John Kavanaugh, *Following Christ in a Consumer Society: the Spirituality of Cultural Resistance,* revised edition (New York: Orbis Books, 1991), p.165.

10. *L'Osservatore Romano* (English edition), 28 June 1982.

11. Warren, op. cit., pp. 6, 16.

12. Kavanaugh, op. cit., p. 127.

13. Warren, op. cit., p. 13.

14. That a culture can leave us painfully out of contact with our depths is inspired by Michael Kearney's recent book on hospice therapy, *Mortally Wounded* (Dublin: Marino Books, 1996).

15. Charles Taylor, *The Ethics of Authenticity* (Cambridge MA: Harvard University Press, 1991), pp. 100-101.

16. *Clashing Symbols* is the title of my forthcoming book on faith

and culture to published by Darton, Longman and Todd early in 1997. It will re-use and expand some of the arguments outlined here.

Chapter 3: The Place of Theology and Religion in Higher Education

1. Aquinas said that 'we cannot know what God is, but only what he is not'. See *Summa Theologiae* 1a, Q2, art3. He deals with this at more length in *Summa Theologiae* 1a, Q 12 and 13. Rahner wrote: 'The agnosticism of the philistine and of self-important philosophers is only the unsuccessful attempt at the true agnosticism which is required of Christians. For Christians adore in hope and love the incomprehensibility which is called God, and in this their faith transpires'. See 'Justifying Faith in an Agnostic World' in *Theological Investigations* XXI (London: Darton Longman & Todd, 1988), p.136.

2. Bishop Michael Murphy, 'The Irish Church: Its Need of Reassessment' in *The Furrow* Vol.47, January 1996, pp.9-16.

3. 'Teaching Religion' in *The Irish Times,* January 1 & 2 1996, p.15.

4. Matthew O'Donnell, 'Return of Theology', in *Link-Up,* No.76, December 1995, p.34.

5. David Tracy, *Analogical Imagination: Christian Theology and the Culture of Pluralism* (London: SCM Press, 1981), pp.1-46.

6. These and many similar issues are addressed in the pages of the *Irish Ecclesiastical Record.*

7. The problems that arose are analysed in John Coolahan, *Irish Education History and Structure* (Dublin: Institute of Public Administration, 1981), pp.105-128.

8. Michael Nolan, 'Public Funding of Theology in the European Community' in *The Irish Journal of Education* XXIV 1990, pp.3-11. The three new members who have

joined the European Union since this article was written – Austria, Finland and Sweden – also fund theology faculties. The central issue is not whether students are grant-aided, which by and large they are in Ireland as elsewhere, but whether the State funds theology in much the same way as other disciplines.

9. Ibid, p.8.

10. Ibid, p.8.

11. These colleges vary enormously in the courses they offer, the qualifications that are awarded and the level of interaction with the State; at one extreme are the seminaries where students don't even receive grant aid for academic study and at the other extreme are State-controlled colleges where some funding is provided.

12. I have analysed the issues raised here in more detail in 'Text and Experience: The Importance of Hermeneutics for Education' in *Irish Educational Studies,* Vol. 11, 1992, pp.249-265.

13. Even a cursory analysis of catechetical texts demonstrates how seriously they have been informed by theological renewal.

14. Think, for instance, of a film like *Jesus of Montreal* with its close attention to the detail of the original sources and its openness to new ways of expressing and interpreting the Christian message.

15. The task of applying renewed theological interpretations to pastoral structures and policies in Ireland has hardly yet begun. It will eventually lead to enormous change.

16. Bernard Lonergan defined theology as the mediation of religion in a culture. He wrote: 'While theology used to be defined as the science about God, today I believe it is to be defined as reflection on the significance and value of religion in a culture.' See Bernard Lonergan, *Philosophy of God and Theology* (London: Darton Longman and Todd, 1973), p.33.

17. Tracy, op. cit., p.6.

18. As reported in *The Irish Times,* 29 June 1996, p.9.

19. The relationship of the Magisterium and theologians is analysed by Francis A.Sullivan, *Magisterium: Teaching Authority in the Catholic Church* (Dublin: Gill & Macmillan, 1983), pp.174-218.

20. John Henry Newman, 'Sermon on Christian Sympathy' in *Parochial and Plain Sermons,* Vol. V (London: Rivingtons, 1869), pp.126-7.

Chapter 4: The Future of Religion at Post-Primary Level

1. Joseph Ratzinger, *Introduction to Christianity,* translated by J.R. Foster (London: Burns and Oates, 1969).

2. Gerard Manley Hopkins, *The Complete Poems, with Selected Prose,* Introduction by Robert Van de Weyer (London: Fount, 1996).

3. Pádraig Hogan, *The Custody and Courtship of Experience – Western Education in Philosophical Perspective* (Dublin: The Columba Press, 1995).

4. T.S. Eliot, 'The Waste Land', in *Collected Poems 1909-1962* (London: Faber & Faber, 1963, 1975).

5. Pádraig Daly, 'Sagart 3' in *Irish Poetry of Faith and Doubt,* edited by John F. Deane (Dublin: Wolfhound Press, 1990).

6. James Fowler, *Stages of Faith* (London & San Francisco: Harper and Row, 1981).

7. Michael Kearney, *Mortally Wounded – Stories of Soul Pain, Death and Healing* (Dublin: Marino, 1996).

8. Margherita Guidacci, *A Book of Sibyls* (Rowan Tree Press, 1989).

Chapter 5: Whither the Fourth R?

1. *Bunreacht na hÉireann (Constitution of Ireland)* (Dublin: The Stationery Office, 1947).

2. Quoted in *A Parents' Guide to Religion in Public Schools* (Nashville: The Freedom Forum – First Amendment Centre, 1995), p.1.

3. *Primary School Curriculum – Teacher's Handbook Part One* (Dublin: The Stationery Office, 1971), p.23.

4. See David Alvey's *Irish Education – the case for secular reform* (Dublin: Church and State Books, 1992).

5. *Religion in the Public Schools – Guidelines for a growing and changing phenomenon* (New York: The Anti-Defamation League, 1992).

6. Campaign to Separate Church and State Ltd. and Jeremiah Noel Murphy V the Minister for Education and others. The judgement of Mr Justice Costello in the High Court, 17 January 1996, pp.40-41.

7. Ibid., p.32.

8. Ibid., p.2.

9. *Religion in the Public Schools,* op. cit., p.3.

10. Ibid., pp.3-4.

11. Anti-Defamation League Report 1995, unpublished.

12. Mr Justice Costello's judgement, 17 January 1996, pp.25-31.

13. Ibid., p.28.

14. G.White, 'Education and the Constitution: convergence of paradigm and praxis' in *The Irish Jurist,* Vol. XXV-XXVII (1990-92), p.73.

15. The National Education Convention Secretariat (ed. J. Coolahan), *Report on The National Education Convention* (Dublin: Government Publications, 1994), p.28.

16. 'Education and Living' supplement of *The Irish Times,* 23 November 1993.

17. 'Budget '96' – a supplement to *The Irish Times,* 24 January 1996.

18. In J.Mulholland and D.Keogh (editors) *Education in Ireland – For what and for whom?* (Cork and Dublin: Hibernia University Press, 1990), pp.71-72.

19. Áine Hyland, 'The Multi-Denominational Experience in the National School System in Ireland', in *Irish Educational Studies,* Vol 8, No.1, 1989, pp.89-114.

20. *Tuarascáil,* Issue No.4, May 1996 (Dublin: Irish National Teachers' Organisation, 1996).

21. *California '3Rs' Project* pamphlet (Isia Vista, California, 1995).

Chapter 6: Subjects or Architects of Culture? Religious Education and Children's Experience

1. George Gerber, quoted in Daniel Ekstrom, *Access Guide to Pop Culture* (New York: DBM Publications, 1989), p. 8.

2. T. de Brún, & M. O'Reilly-de Brun, in T. Larkin & A. Honan *Windows on the World: Shaping and Being Shaped by Culture* (Navan: Columban Fathers and Sisters, 1992), p. 7.

3. Ibid., p. 8.

4. P. Andrews, *Changing Children: Living With a New Generation* (Dublin: Gill & Macmillan, 1994).

5. In A. Shorter, *Toward a Theology of Inculturation* (London: Geoffrey Chapman, 1988), p. 35ff.

6. W. M. Watt, *Religious Truth for our Time* (Oxford: One World Press, 1995), p. 13ff.

7. Ibid.

8. A. Rich, from the poem 'Natural Resources' in *The Dream of a Common Language* (New York: W.W. Norton & Co., 1978).

9. B. Thorne, (1986) 'Girls and Boys Together ... but mostly apart: Gender arrangements in elementery school' in M.S. Kimmel & M.A. Messner (eds.) *Men's Lives* (Boston: Allyn & Bacon, 1995), p. 61.

10. K. Mc Donnell, *Kid Culture: Children and Adults and Popular Culture,* (Toronto: Second Story Press, 1994), p. 51.

11. Ibid.

12. W. Wink, 'The Myth of Redemptive Violence: Exposing the Roots of 'Might Makes Right" in *Sojourners,* April 1992, pp. 18-22.

13. D. Goleman, *Emotional Intelligence – Why it can matter more than I.Q.* (London: Bloomsbury, 1996).

14. K. Walsh & M. Walsh, 'Problems of Adult Religious Education' in *The Month,* March 1983, pp. 92-96.

15. D. Murray, 'The Language of Catechesis' in D.A. Lane (ed.) *Religious Education and the Future* (Dublin: Columba Press, 1986), p. 129.

16. Ibid., p. 133.

Afterword

1. Simone Weil, *The Need for Roots* (New York: Harper & Row, 1952), p. 43.

2. *The Pastoral Constitution on the Church in the Modern World,* nn. 4, 32, 43.

3. Ibid., n. 44.

4. *Decree on Ecumenism,* n. 3.

5. Ibid., n. 1.

6. Ibid., n. 3.

7. Ibid., n. 6.

8. *Declaration on the Relationship of the Church to non-Christian Religions,* n. 2; *Pastoral Constitution on the Church in the Modern World,* n. 92.

9. *Decree on the Missionary Activity of the Church,* n. 3; *Dogmatic Constitution on the Church,* n. 16.

10. *Declaration on the Relationship of the Church to non-Christian Religions,* n. 2.

11. *Ut Unum Sint,* n. 20.

12. *Decree on Ecumenism,* n. 4.

13. Unpublished Presidential Address, May 1996.

14. *Pastoral Constitution on the Church in the Modern World,* n. 92.

15. Ibid.

NOTES ON THE CONTRIBUTORS

Michael Paul Gallagher is an Irish Jesuit, previously a lecturer in English Literature at University College Dublin, who now teaches fundamental theology at the Gregorian University, Rome. His most recent books are: *What are they saying about Unbelief?* (New York: Paulist Press, 1995), *Free to Believe,* revised edition (London: Darton, Longman and Todd, 1996), *Questions of Faith* (Dublin: Veritas, 1996).

Michael Drumm is a priest of the Diocese of Elphin. He is Head of the Department of Systematic Theology at the Mater Dei Institute of Education and is an occasional lecturer in Theology in the Pontifical University, St Patrick's College, Maynooth, and in St Angela's College, Sligo. He has lectured widely on adult religious education programmes throughout Ireland and is attached to the parish of St Mary's, Haddington Road, Dublin.

Ann Walsh teaches in the CBS Secondary School, Kilkenny. She is author of *Reason to Believe* and *Believe to Live,* two titles in the Believing and Living series in religious education for post-primary schools (Dublin: Veritas, 1994, 1995). She is a member of the Religious Education Course Committee of the National Council for Curriculum and Assessment, which is designing new programmes for the junior and senior cycles of post-primary school. She is also a member of the Standing Committee of the Association of Secondary Teachers, Ireland.

Kieran Griffin has been Principal of the Bray School Project since the school was opened in 1981. Prior to that, he was Director of the Blackrock Teachers' Centre. He has served on the Education Committee of the Irish National Teachers' Organisation and has been involved in carrying out research surveys commissioned by the INTO into various aspects of primary education. He is Chairman of the NCCA Course Committee for Visual Arts in the primary curriculum. As Principal of one of the first inter-denominational schools in the Republic, he has worked actively with parents in developing managerial procedures and curricula which reflect inter-denominational principles in education.

Tom Larkin is a primary teacher in Scoil Cholmcille, Donaghmede. He worked for a number of years on educational projects with the Society of St. Columbans and is co-author of a number of publications produced by the Columbans for schools, including the Windows on the World series for primary schools and the Gateway series for post-primary schools. He is an adviser to the Episcopal Commission on Catechetics and is a member of its sub-group for the primary sector.

Kevin Williams is a lecturer in education at the Mater Dei Institute, Dublin. He has written on philosophical issues in Irish and international journals and is the author/editor of several books, including *Understanding Trade Unions* (Dublin: O'Brien Press, 1990) and *Assessment: A Discussion Paper* (Dublin: ASTI, 1992). He is currently President of the Educational Studies Association of Ireland.

Dermot A. Lane is President of Mater Dei Institute of Education, Parish Priest of Balally, Dublin, and a part-time lecturer in the Irish School of Ecumenics in Dublin. He is author of several books of theology, including *Christ at the Centre: Selected Issues in Christology* (Dublin: Veritas, 1990), *Keeping Hope Alive: Stirrings in Christian Theology* (Dublin: Gill & Macmillan, 1996), and is one of the editors of *The New Dictionary of Theology* (Dublin: Gill & Macmillan, 1988).

Pádraig Hogan, a former President of the ESAI, is a lecturer in Education in Maynooth College, and has spoken and published frequently on educational issues in Ireland and abroad. He was General Editor of the journal *Irish Educational Studies* from 1990-94 and was Guest Editor for the inaugural issue of the ASTI's new journal *Issues in Education* (Dublin: ASTI, 1996). He is author of the book *The Custody and Courtship of Experience – Western Education in Philosophical Perspective* (Dublin: Columba Press, 1996).